W9-AYZ-512

Law as a Career:

■ A Practical

Guide

The Law School Admission Council is a nonprofit association of United States and Canadian law schools. Law School Admission Services administers the Council's programs and provides services to the legal education community.

LSAT® and the Law Services logo are registered by Law School Admission Services, Inc. Law School Forum is a service mark of Law School Admission Services, Inc. *The Official LSAT PrepTest*, *The Official LSAT PrepKit*, and *The Official LSAT TriplePrep* are trademarks of Law School Admission Services, Inc.

Copyright © 1993 by Law School Admission Services, Inc.

All rights reserved. This book may not be reproduced or transmitted, in whole or in part, by any means, electronic or mechanical, including photocopying, recording, or by any information storage and retrieval system, without permission of the publisher. For information, write: Publications, Law School Admission Services, Box 40, 661 Penn Street, Newtown, PA 18940.

Law School Admission Services fees, policies and procedures relating to, but not limited to, test registration, test administration, test score reporting, misconduct, and other matters may change without notice at any time. To remain up to date on Law School Admission Services policies and procedures, you may obtain a current *LSAT/LSDAS Registration and Information Book,* or you may contact our candidate service representatives.

ISBN 0-942639-40-5

Table of Contents

- **Introduction**
  - Chapter 1   Choosing Law as a Career 4
  - Chapter 2   Lawyering: What's It Really Like? 17
  - Chapter 3   The Experience of Law School:
               What You Can Expect 24
  - Chapter 4   Gaining Admission to Law School:
               Preparation and Self-assessment 30
  - Chapter 5   Gathering Information about Law Schools 45
  - Chapter 6   Evaluating Law Schools 51
  - Chapter 7   Selecting and Applying to Law Schools 67
  - Chapter 8   Paying for Law School: Financial Aid
               and Debt Management 82
  - Chapter 9   The Admission Process:
               What You Need to Know 87
  - Chapter 10   After Law School: Taking the Bar
               Exam and Finding a Job 94
  - Chapter 11   Getting Started 98

- **Appendices**
  - Appendix A   Differences between ABA-approved
               and Non-ABA-approved Law Schools 99
  - Appendix B   U.S. Law Schools Approved by the American
               Bar Association 103
  - Appendix C   Canadian Member Law Schools 114
  - Appendix D   LSAC Statement of Good Admission Practices . . 116
  - Appendix E   Prelaw Readings: Books of Interest 125
  - Appendix F   Geographic Guide to Law Schools in the
               United States (by region) 133
  - Appendix G   Geographic Guide to Canadian Law Schools . . . 155

- **Index** 158

Introduction

Perhaps you come from a long line of lawyers and everyone in your family expects you to become a lawyer, but you still don't know if it's for you.

Perhaps you've been out of school now for a while, working—in business, in the arts or education, or in a technical field—and you're planning, or simply dreaming about, a career change. Could it be law that will fit the bill?

You may be at the end of your college years with no clear idea of what to do next. You like school, you're undecided about a career—could law school be a move in the right direction?

You might be just beginning college now—maybe you're still in high school—and you want to prepare yourself for a future in the law, or explore it as a possibility.

Your thoughts about law school may lead you to any number of conclusions. Law school is not for everyone, but it may be perfect for you—and you may not even know it yet! If you are going to make an informed decision, you should have all the facts. You certainly should not choose to pursue law, nor should you reject the possibility out of hand, before you know what it's all about; that includes having a realistic picture of what it means to be a lawyer, what it's like to attend law school, and what it will involve to prepare for a career in the law. Included in that last category is information you will need to make clear-headed and thoughtful personal choices about the law schools that are best for you—as well as information pertaining to the very practical logistics of completing the paperwork properly and financing your legal education.

Wherever you are on the continuum of thinking about law school, this book will help you clarify your thoughts on the matter, perhaps debunk some of your misconceptions, or even open your eyes to ideas you've not considered before. It's a long road from your first consideration of law school to a successful career in the law; it involves a serious commitment of time, money, and personal resources at the outset, and perseverance all along the way.

In this book, we take a look at who actually chooses law and why, exploring the myths and the facts that lead to that choice. We examine the value of a legal education, so you can decide whether you might be someone who will benefit from traveling that particular path. We also help you take a realistic look at your own chances of acceptance, offering guidance in how to make choices that may enhance your chances, how to prepare for the law school admission test, and how to effectively fill out a law school application.

Law school applicants are not—nor should they be—concerned only with being selected, but also with their own evaluation and selection of a law school to attend. There are 191 ABA-approved law schools in the United States and Canada; this book advises you about an important part of the application process—narrowing your selection to schools that best fit your needs.

Of course, successful completion of law school and the subsequent passing of the state bar exam are only the beginning. In order to fully realize your dream, you need a job, not just a degree; therefore, it is wise to look ahead to life after graduation. The good news is that there are many directions from which to choose. We discuss the range of these opportunities in this book as well.

Many students are concerned with how they will be able to finance a law school education; the numbers can be overwhelming when you see them on paper. It is important to know that, each year, many students complete their law school education even though they are not independently wealthy and they did not plan and save for law school since childhood. Financial aid officers work very hard to help prospective students assess their resources and obtain loans to meet their financial obligation. This includes students who already have a school debt to repay as well as older applicants who have long-standing financial obligations—such as children and a mortgage—pressing on them. Financing a law school education can be a challenge—and it can present you with some tough decisions to make—but in no case should you assume before you even begin that it is financially out of reach.

Finally, we have tried to anticipate the most commonly asked questions by minority men and women interested in the law, and also by prospective applicants who have disabilities. For further information, we refer you to specific organizations and educational resources, and we urge you to seek out individuals who may have shared your concerns.

For up-to-date insights and perspectives, we've gleaned the wisdom and tapped the experience of numerous professionals who work closely with students at every point along the way: prelaw advisors at undergraduate institutions, law school admission officers, financial aid and career services personnel, and law faculty, among others. Occasionally we have quoted particular points of view that we believe represent a consensus of these professionals.

Whether your undergraduate college years are still ahead of you, or just behind you; whether you've been in a profession other than law for 10 or 20 years or have never held a full-time job in your life, this book will help you consider law as a direction that may be right for you.

Chapter 1

Choosing Law as a Career

Who Chooses Law and Why?

There is no one path that leads to law school, and there is no perfect time to decide to become a lawyer. Individuals bring a variety of backgrounds, a multiplicity of perspectives, and, certainly, differing misconceptions to the prospect of a future in the law.

In any career path, there are many avenues that steer people in a particular direction. There are, for example, those people who seem to know from very early on in their lives what they want to do when they grow up, and there are those who seem to move from one endeavor to another—for years after their friends have found their particular niches—before being willing or able to make a serious commitment to a vocation.

On the one hand, law has attracted individuals who turn to this pursuit after a period of indecision, or after working in another field for a number of years. On the other hand, there are lawyers who, by virtue of their familiarity with the profession from an early age, seem to be fulfilling a destiny that has patiently awaited them since childhood. Each of these paths has its own benefits and drawbacks. In addition to individual circumstances, all of us who live in the modern world are beset by a plethora of images of who a lawyer is and what a lawyer does; these images come to us through the media and through our own observations. It's easy to point to the television and movie lawyers and say sagely, "Yes, we know that's the glamorous side and not a realistic picture." But we don't always remember that law is such a broad-ranging profession that to know one lawyer, or to have close contact with one law firm, in no way gives us a full picture of the profession of law.

Whether you've come to consider the legal profession for yourself only recently, or you've been considering it for a long time, there are advantages and disadvantages that each particular perspective brings to bear on the life-altering decision to attend law school. Let us take a look at some of the more common directions from which individuals arrive at this conclusion. Perhaps you will recognize yourself—or some part of yourself—in one of the descriptions that follows. If you are completely sure that law school is for you, congratulations! You may want to move directly to the more practical sections of this book, or you may want to read on to find out more about who your prospective classmates will be.

■ *My Father, Mother, or Cousin Is A Lawyer, So I Guess I'll Be One Too*

Those of you who feel like you've been groomed your entire life to enter the family profession have a particularly strong responsibility to assess yourself honestly and realistically. You will do no one any good—not yourself and not your family—by entering a profession for which you are ill-suited in order to please someone else and fulfill the expectations of others. On the other hand, if you indeed are drawn to the law for all the right reasons, you are among the fortunate. You are fortunate to have an insider's perspective close at hand. Notice we said *close at hand*, not *by osmosis*. You will still benefit by exploring the reality of a lawyer's life by direct observation or perhaps through working at a part-time job. Insight is not automatically conferred upon you by virtue of having a lawyer in the family. While making full use of your contacts, bear in mind that observing *one* kind of law practice only gives you a part of the picture. If you are interested in the kind of law, or the type of law practice, to which you have ready access, so much the better. But it would be wise not to assume that is all there is to the law. As far as assessing yourself as a likely candidate for a career in law, you would do well to ask yourself the same kinds of questions that anyone coming to law by a less direct route should ask of himself or herself. These questions are discussed in the next section.

■ *I'm a Senior or Junior in College and I'm Undecided About My Life*

Although one may begin to think about being a lawyer as early as high school or in the first two years of college, many prospective law school students begin to target law school during the last half of their college career. There are some in this group who—when confronted with the dilemma of choosing a career path—rapidly become convinced that law school should be their next step; all signs point to it when they begin seriously to pin down their aspirations for the future, and their teachers will perhaps concur. It is still useful for those students to periodically reevaluate their goals to be sure law is really what they want.

Then there are those who are looking for ways to remain in the safe harbor of academia rather than face the real world and look for a job. Those students, if they are bright (and sometimes even if they're not) will consider medical school, business school, and other graduate programs, along with law school. Since law school is widely considered the closest thing available to a continuation of the liberal arts degree, some students will choose it by default. These students too must take a closer look, particularly at what law school entails—intellectually, psychologically, and financially— before beginning the long and demanding process of applying to law school. It's possible that such a student will make a good candidate for law school and a successful lawyer, but he or she must first think this choice through carefully, using as many resources as are available. Law school is too serious a proposition to be undertaken by default alone. Legal study requires a major commitment of time and money; it will require many hours of serious study.

Most college juniors and seniors considering law school will fall somewhere in the middle of the continuum between the dabbler and the already dedicated. You probably know who you are. You've been told you are bright and you can talk anyone into anything. Intelligence is, of course, a factor—but there are all kinds of intelligence. The kind of intelligence required for success in law school, and in law as a discipline, has to do with your analytical powers, your ability to reason and approach problems logically, your verbal and communication skills, and your good judgment. You must be able to read and write well *before* you enter law school and you must be able to analyze diverse bodies of information to reach logical, viable solutions. Learning how to advocate a particular point of view within the context of the legal system can be both stimulating and frustrating. Being an effective lawyer calls for a fair amount of intellectual dexterity—the ability to juggle three or four ideas simultaneously. Skills in interacting with all kinds of people are also important. Depending on the kind of law you practice, you will deal with people from a variety of cultural backgrounds, professions, income levels, needs, and interests. Some of your relationships will be very rewarding, both professionally and personally. Others may seem difficult—if not distasteful. In any case, you must be willing and able to offer intelligent competent counsel to all of your clients: the practice of law is a service profession.

Native intelligence and communication skills, however, are not going to be enough. Staying power is also necessary. There are some very intelligent people who do not have the ability or are not willing to stay focused, to maintain the discipline required to absorb large quantities of information, and to persevere. There are others who are not geniuses, but who succeed in law school because they are dedicated and willing to work hard.

Jim Riley, prelaw advisor at Regis University in Denver, puts it succinctly: "Whether you succeed or not will depend on your persistently doing the work that is necessary on a daily basis ... I have had students who have been less than brilliant—(who were) average—but who worked as hard as the dickens to get the job done. That willingness to work hard and pursue the hard chore, and get it done, **that** is much more important than intellectual brilliance. Once you have that ability to persist, it's going to stay with you (throughout your entire career)."

What other characteristics are a good match for someone considering law school? Margot Baker, a prelaw advisor who talks to students at Southern Methodist University in Dallas, cites the following typical answers that demonstrate to her that someone is on the right track: "I love learning new things. I love reading about new things." She is wary of what she calls the "external affirmation" that exists in students who have been told by others that because they're argumentative, or good at persuasion, or good at writing, they qualify as candidates for law school. Students should probe themselves for the internal counterpart to those characteristics, asking themselves: Do I think those are good descriptors of me? What other traits do I have that I'd want to use in a job?

The junior or senior who is seriously considering law must not only assess personal attributes and take a full measure of personal goals, but also look closely at his or her academic credentials. It's not enough to know you're good at writing; you will need to have some documentation of your abilities in this area. This is where grades and course selection come into play; we devote more time to that subject later in this book. As you begin to get more serious, you will have to give some considered thought to the taking of the Law School Admission Test (LSAT). All law schools presently approved by the American Bar Association (ABA) or the Federation of Law Societies of Canada (FLSC) require students to take the LSAT as part of the admission process. (On rare occasions, an exception may be made for people with certain disabilities.) You must also begin to research actively the details of what it is to be a lawyer (see Chapter 2) through talking to lawyers, reading books on the subject, or perhaps working at a law firm. Many colleges have prelaw advisors who can be of enormous assistance to you, and who can possibly put you in touch with lawyers in the area if you don't have any contacts of your own.

Opinions differ on the question of whether you should begin law school with a sure sense of your direction after you earn your law degree. Frequently, persons coming to law school with a career direction in mind change it as a result of certain courses, professors, and programs, and some students with no particular career path in mind discover one. There is no question that the education you will get in law school is invaluable, no matter what your long-term career goals are—or what fate has in store for you.

"Legal education," says Joseph Burns, prelaw advisor at Boston College, "teaches you to think precisely, to think through the implications of things clearly, and to make an argument—and that's an education, a training, that is valuable in *any* career."

Susan Meyerowitz, prelaw advisor at the University of Rochester in New York, refers to legal training as "the last generalist professional degree." Donald Racheter, director of the prelaw program at the Central University of Iowa, points out that as an "extension of the liberal arts preparation," a law degree is useful preparation for a range of careers, including education, business, and government service. Nevertheless, others are more cautious on this point: Margot Baker at Southern Methodist University assesses those who pursue a legal education without some notion of "wanting to use it for something" as indulging in "a pretty expensive pastime." She concurs with other prelaw advisors, however, when she makes it clear that "people who go to law school often wind up doing some pretty wonderful things" even if they weren't certain about their goals when they first entered law school.

- *I've Been at My Job for Two Years (or Five or Ten) and I'm Ready for a Change*

It's not unusual to find law school candidates who have been out of school for a while, and who did not matriculate immediately following their graduation from college. Some have been out of school for just a year; often these are students who considered law school earlier, but were not quite ready to make the commitment at that time. There is nothing sacred about attending law school right after graduating college. You should not assume that an educational career or life experience that is unconventional, or reflective of a diverse background, will automatically be prejudicial to your cause. To the contrary, it may enhance your cause. Some admission officers, in fact, applaud the decision to work for a few years first, acknowledging that such "time out" from school may provide important life experiences that enhance your understanding and maturation.

Once you enter law school, however, there is no waffling. A legal education will demand the best of you, and if you don't have a clear commitment when you begin, it's going to be very difficult to keep your focus and succeed in mastering the program of study. Naturally, some who intended only to delay law school by a year never do go back; they may find success in some other endeavor. Others will be happy with whatever they choose as an alternative to law school *for a while*, but the dream of law school comes back to haunt them, prod at them, and ultimately inspire them to follow their original ambition after all. Those who decide to return after five years or more can rest assured that they will find the company of many other students in their age bracket; it's not unusual for an entering law school class to be made up of students in their twenties, thirties, forties, and even older.

Among this group of returning students there are those who are intent upon using their law degree to enhance their current profession. You may be a certified public accountant who intends to become a tax attorney, or an engineer or scientist interested in patent law, or perhaps you are someone in health care—a doctor or nurse—who is drawn to environmental law because of the impact of the environment on the health of our citizens. For some, it's a question of "maxing out" at a certain income level in a chosen profession; for others it's the need to be continually challenged that spurs a successful professional to undertake the rigors of law school.

If an expected higher salary is a factor, you should probably find out if your expectation is realistic by talking to other people in your field who have gone for the law degree. Do not just assume that your income level will rise. Think also about how easy or difficult it will be to get back into your field after taking time off for law school; this may be a case where a part-time schedule is appropriate.

Most returning students are individuals who are dissatisfied with their current career or who are moving into a new stage of life and very much want to transform their lives: they seek a change of venue, a change of faces, a change of tasks. Some have raised families and are now looking to begin or resume a career. Some who feel underutilized in their current positions are determined to advance themselves professionally; they understand law to be an area that requires some mental muscle. There are also those individuals who work in highly technical fields, and who—according to Fredi Miller, director of admissions and financial aid at the University of Pittsburgh—"have found themselves very restricted (due to their lack of) people contact."

For those of you who are dissatisfied with your work and believe that law is where you really want to be, it is particularly important that you get a clear idea of what lawyering is, and how the job description may vary according to the type of law you practice (see Chapter 2) so that you don't have unrealistic expectations. Bonnie Saito, placement officer at Whittier College in Los Angeles, gives an example of the individual who didn't enjoy his current position because, he said, "it required too much reading and writing"—clearly, law may not be the right direction for that person because both law school and the law profession require a good deal of both. Even for that person, however, the realistic career possibilities after law school are worth exploring; there are positions that characteristically require less reading and writing than others. "Some people dislike their current situation so much they'll do anything to get out of it," says Saito.

There are also those who have been backed into a corner by circumstances beyond their control and who *must* explore new career possibilities and ultimately land on one they can live with. Baker calls these the "reluctant career changers" and cites examples in the Texas area: "People who've been in the oil and gas business; people who've been in real estate ... people reading the handwriting on the wall and who, though they haven't been laid off, are saying to themselves, 'There's no future here, let me think about my second alternative.' "

It's probably worth pointing out here that along with concerns about fitting in because of age, returning students often wonder whether they will be admitted to law school, especially if their academic record is not recent, and not as outstanding as they would wish. In Chapter 7, we discuss how you can make the most of your application. Your years in the job force or raising a family may work in your favor; some admission officers may see this as a reflection of maturity and stability, and a balancing factor in the overall picture.

One special feature of the returning student is this: Whereas students who choose law school immediately after college often see it as an opportunity to move to another city, post-college students—who may have put down roots in terms of jobs, families, or ownership of a home—often prefer to stay closer to home. Those who do elect to move may have different concerns with respect to relocation; for example, they may need to know about schools for their children or job possibilities for a spouse. When it comes time to make such decisions, an admission office can often direct you to information sources. But it would be wise to talk to other returning students, even earlier on, who may have made similar choices and who can guide you in your thinking and planning.

■ *Is Law School for Me?*

Maybe you are someone who has only recently begun to consider law school; maybe it's only a tiny spark, a buried thought that hasn't even come to fruition yet. If so, you will want to ask yourself where that spark came from. See if you can clarify your thinking. What inspired you to consider law school in the first place? Was it a person, an event, an experience, a problem, an aspiration, a desire? Give some thought to recalling, sharpening, and refining your answer to this question. Perhaps your motivation is based on an idea you have formed about what lawyers do, the kind of salary they earn, or the power that lawyers are thought to exercise in our society—their capacity to change things, to help people, to solve problems, to make a difference, or to exert influence. Many lawyers are certainly drawn to the profession because of some combination of these ideas and ideals. But broad impressions are not a sound basis for making a decision that will require a major investment of your resources—personal and financial. It is important, therefore, that you take a close look at the profession today and assess just how close your ideals measure against the reality.

Ask yourself what it is about being a lawyer or a law-trained person that interests you. How does being a lawyer fit in with your needs and your career goals? You must spend some time and energy exploring your own particular reasons for wanting to study law, and you need to examine the real truth behind any assumptions you have made. The next section, "Reasons People Choose Law" will help you begin to do this.

If any of the following activities interest you, you may be looking in the right direction when looking toward law: debating, expressing ideas clearly, reading and studying, assembling and developing facts, probing issues and problems to find basic premises or solutions, and conducting interviews to obtain information. Similarly, if you are interested in social and human problems, governmental and political arrangements, or the art of negotiating, you may wish to study law. If you are articulate in both speaking and writing, and you enjoy the dispute, argument, and resolution of conflict, the study of law may offer you the satisfaction you seek in a career.

Good communication skills are among the most important characteristics for aspiring law school applicants. Besides the requisite "good reading and writing skills," the following skills are equally important: reading with comprehension and speed; proofreading/editing effectively; thinking quickly under pressure; analyzing and synthesizing information; writing with precision; writing persuasively; interviewing effectively; listening accurately; and speaking convincingly. Some of these skills are grounded in natural ability, though most are honed through the rigorous academic study available during your college years, or over a period of time working at certain kinds of jobs. In any case, you will ultimately need to demonstrate some aspect of these skills when making your case for acceptance to law school. (See Chapter 7 for more on applying to law school.)

In addition, you will, of course, have to take a realistic look at your credentials, and assess yourself with the kind of barometer that will be used by admission officers at the law schools to which you will ultimately apply. In most cases, you must first complete four years of an undergraduate college education (although there are some schools that will accept you after three years of college under a program permitting you to obtain an undergraduate degree while at law school). The details of how your college's reputation, your own standing in your class, and your performance on the Law School Admission Test affect your chances for law school admission will be discussed in greater detail later in this book.

The remainder of this chapter is devoted to a closer look at the reasons people choose law; we explore the myths and the facts behind each of these reasons. We discuss the overall benefits of a legal education as well.

The Reasons People Choose Law

■ *Intellectual Stimulation*

As we said earlier, legal study and practice may challenge your abilities to reason, analyze, and communicate as they may never have been challenged before. Additionally, you'll be able to further your legal education and refine your skills through the camaraderie of your colleagues and through the various publications and associations with which you'll be involved. You may even work on a case that sets a legal precedent. At the same time, you should know that a good portion of legal work is often tedious, repetitive, and downright boring. For example, it's not uncommon for a lawyer to spend hours poring over thousands of pages of background material to research a case, or filling out the same kinds of forms day after day. Be prepared for both the excitement and the monotony.

■ *Financial Reward*

Many students choose law because of its reputation for offering a financially rewarding career. There's no doubt about it: You may make a lot of money as an attorney. But too many individuals have unrealistic expectations in this area. Ilona DeRemer, assistant dean at Gonzaga University in Spokane, contends that this area of lawyers and money is fraught with "serious misconception ... particularly in terms of salary ranges, variances between geographic areas, types of positions, and so on." Many students she has spoken to, she says, are surprised when she tells them that the higher-range salaries are almost exclusively the province of large firms in larger cities, and that only a small percentage of law school graduates go that route.

Prelaw advisor Susan Meyerowitz at the University of Rochester asks her students—if it is money that motivates them—if they are willing to put in the time it takes to make that kind of money. "There are long hours if you're going for the high ticket," she warns them. "No one gives you that kind of money for nothing."

Let's suppose you are an excellent student, and your goal is to help the indigent, or work in a district attorney's office, or establish a private practice in a local community (as do roughly half the lawyers in the United States). You can expect to earn a significantly lower salary than those individuals working in the big corporations in the larger cities—not only at the start of your career but quite possibly throughout your years of practice. There is nothing wrong with wanting to make a lot of money as a lawyer; just be sure your goals are realistic.

■ *Effecting Social Change*

Joining the legal profession is one of the most effective ways to bring about social change. It can be especially valuable to those who seek the opportunity to work within the legal system to reform social injustice. At the same time, the legal system can be a source of great frustration, because real change takes years to accomplish. If you intend to study and practice law with the goal of changing the status quo in any area, you will have to supplement your expert legal skill with all the patience, determination, persistence, and political savvy you can summon.

■ *Prestige*

As a lawyer, you may work for a prominent Wall Street law firm, defend or prosecute a notorious person, serve as judge, and get elected to public office. Even so, our society regards the legal profession with ambivalence. On the one hand, lawyers are esteemed for their esoteric knowledge and expertise. On the other hand, they are often mistrusted and sometimes seen as cold, calculating scoundrels who are motivated only by greed and power. It pays to be aware that not everyone will appreciate or respect the skills you worked so long and hard to achieve.

General Benefits of a Legal Education

As we discussed earlier, the study of law is the most generic of all professional postgraduate disciplines. A legal education teaches you to read for a clear grasp of content and relationships, to analyze and solve problems creatively in concrete situations, and to advocate and persuade orally and in writing. Whether or not a person chooses to practice law specifically, a legal education is clearly excellent training for almost any professional position. In Chapter 2, we briefly discuss the variety of positions possible for a person who has a legal education, including the various organizational settings in which lawyers may find themselves. Besides the conventional avenues for lawyering jobs, many more general professions such as banking, insurance, real estate, securities, government, education, and international trade—to name just a few—are significant areas of employment for law school graduates.

Getting More Information

By now you may have a better idea where you fit in the wide-ranging category of "people who want to be lawyers." You understand that people come to this decision from many different perspectives and are persuaded by an array of information that is not always reliable. If you are thinking about becoming a lawyer, then you should by all means take the next step in exploring the possibilities: gather more information. But get your information from people who know. If you are in high school, talk to your school counselor. You will, at the very least, want to prepare yourself scholastically by adhering to a rigorous academic curriculum so you can begin to think about choosing an appropriate college. If you are already in college, you may want to seek out prelaw advisors at your school.

If you now are working, go directly to the source: the admission offices of law schools in your area. Talk to lawyers as well, if possible. Begin to explore the world of law, whenever and wherever you can. Talk to friends, family, and colleagues. You will find your ideas taking shape and taking on an importance when you speak them aloud in a way that they never can when they remain hidden in the private reaches of your mind.

Career services and alumni offices at law schools are all possible resources for finding names of people you may call, if you don't know anyone personally or through a reference. If it's possible to work in a law setting for a time, you may clarify your own sense of what it is to be a lawyer and what you may want to do in your own career.

Any inside information you can get that will help you clarify your thinking can only end up helping you when you begin the process of persuading an admission committee that you are a worthy candidate for their law school. Bear in mind, however, that it is still your academic record that takes precedence and, next, any personal accomplishments in which you demonstrated initiative and leadership capabilities. These aspects of law school preparation will be discussed more extensively in Chapter 4.

Finally, a question that comes up repeatedly, even by those who themselves are considering law as a profession, is: do we really need more lawyers? Aren't there too many lawyers already? Like any profession or any employment area, there is always room for another *qualified* member. You may have to adjust your plans concerning the practice area you had hoped to enter; you may have to live in a part of the country that you didn't plan to live in at the outset of your career. But if you graduate from law school, do reasonably well, and maintain a flexible attitude, you will find that there is a place for you in the legal profession. For a closer look at what the profession might actually entail, turn to Chapter 2.

Chapter 2

Lawyering: What's It Really Like?

The Misconceptions

Popular television shows might lead you to believe that a lawyer's work revolves around courtroom dramatics. Movies also would have us believe that all law is trial law—with a few days put aside for a meeting with a client who's in jail. Nothing could be further from the truth.

The great majority of a lawyer's work is done *outside the courtroom.* Many lawyers do not litigate at all. The point of a great deal of lawyering is to keep clients out of the kind of trouble that might bring them into the courtroom—and to the extent that the courtroom can be avoided, the lawyer is successfully doing his or her job. Despite the commonly held misapprehension that the lawyer is a litigious adversary, a lawyer is more often concerned with securing harmonious and orderly arrangements, and with avoiding and settling controversy, especially in regard to the drafting of contracts, wills, and other such documents. Legal skill and expertise often come into play in the necessary supervision of the complex relationships of human beings and their organizations—corporations, unions, cities, states, federal departments and agencies, cultural organizations, and international associations. Many lawyers preside over the financing and operation of business, both to ensure its operation in accordance with corporate law and to advance entrepreneurial goals.

Law school applicants often assume that they will go to work for a law firm following their completion of law school. However, about 23 percent of all lawyers practice outside of law firms. This includes about 9.8 percent who work in private industry and for private associations; about 8 percent employed by the government; about 2.7 percent working in the judiciary; and about 2 percent in a variety of other positions, including public interest law and education.

Lawyer specialization is also a source of some misunderstanding among prelaw students. Law school education is broad-ranging; most lawyers don't become involved in a specialty until after they have worked in the profession for several years, and their specialty then becomes a function of the expertise they have developed by working on certain types of cases repeatedly. However, the generalist lawyer appears to be on the wane; as society becomes more complex, many law firms are relying on lawyers who have expertise in a specific area. Some schools offer opportunities to achieve some expertise in a particular area for those students who feel prepared to make long-term career decisions early on; there are also educators who believe students are better off keeping their options open as long as possible.

What Lawyers Actually Do

The practice of law is multifaceted, and the more you explore the particulars of each setting and how that setting best suits your own needs and goals, the less likely you are to feel trapped in an environment you could have avoided had you bothered to learn what that environment was like. You may have a personal preference for the more social or for the more secluded aspects of a law career, but you will need to be adept at both. Certain settings are likely to involve you more directly with clients; other environments may offer the prospect that you will eventually be appreciated and rewarded for your intellect. If effecting change in society is what you're after, you may have to be satisfied with incremental change. Keep in mind that lawyers also can effect change for an individual client.

Lawyers are found just about everywhere in a society as complex as ours. A typical first job for a lawyer might be setting up an individual practice; working in a law firm or a corporate legal department; entering government service at the local, state, or federal level; accepting a judicial clerkship; joining a bank, trust company, or accounting firm; or working for a public interest group. Following is a list—though not a comprehensive one—of some of the specialties within the law profession: corporate law, antitrust law, intellectual property law, family law, tax law, labor law, criminal law, public interest law, international law, securities law, environmental law, real estate, estate law, tort law, and bankruptcy law. Other areas of specialty exist and often are more prevalent in some parts of the country than others; there is quite a bit of overlap in specialty areas as well. New areas of expertise, such as banking, health services, and sports law continue to develop to accommodate our rapidly changing world; a lawyer may develop a well-defined subspecialty by accumulating a high volume of a specific kind of case that may recur. The law school's career services office can provide you with more information on these specific practice areas.

Different Settings in Which to Practice Law

Aside from varying subject-matter specialties, there are a number of practice settings in which a lawyer can exercise his or her skills. There are more lawyers in solo practices and small firms, but the rapid growth of the big firms and the well publicized starting salaries of newly minted lawyers have received a great deal of publicity in recent years. These positions actually represent only a small fraction of the available positions for lawyers. Beginning with a closer look at these large firms—with their advantages and their disadvantages—we offer a description of the diverse settings in which a lawyer may work over the course of a career.

■ *The Large Law Firm*

A large firm, sometimes referred to as a national firm, is comprised of 100 to 200 partners (sometimes more) and associates, often with two or more offices. Generally, these firms are located near the financial communities and Fortune 500 companies of major metropolitan areas. The nature of the legal work undertaken by a national firm might range from preparing the initial articles of incorporation and bylaws for a new enterprise to handling a corporate reorganization under the provisions of federal bankruptcy laws. The firm may be involved in a huge corporate lawsuit that will take years to resolve, or it may be working on the details of a multimillion-dollar business transaction.

The new associate's work is likely to be restricted to a small, structured group. Usually large firms are segmented into specialty groups such as litigation, corporate, real estate, trusts and estates, and so on. Sometimes associates rotate from one department to another. The associate's work at the outset consists of supplying background research for the more senior members, or writing simple legal documents or shorter portions of more complicated documents. Associates also proofread, oversee the mechanical aspects of preparing legal documents in the appropriate form, and serve as general assistants as needed. It may be some years before associates are given primary responsibility for a case. Competition for advancement can be quite intense. An associate will usually leave, or be eased out, if it becomes clear that he or she will not become a partner, although today many nonpartners stay on as senior associates or nonequity partners. Partnership selection typically begins about the seventh year. Although these large firms are likely to pay quite well, they do expect a lot from their associates for that compensation.

There are also regional firms that are smaller than the national firms but more sophisticated than the typical smaller firm (discussed below). These regional firms may offer some of the benefits of each. The work may be more challenging than in a small firm, but there may not be quite as much client contact. Typical clients might be a regional corporation for whom the firm might serve as both business and legal adviser, or a private individual or family who demands a high level of service. The lines between such regional firms and national firms are increasingly blurred as many regional firms are absorbed by or evolve into national firms.

■ *Small Firms/Solo Practice*

The smaller the firm, the more local its practice. A small practice may handle routine family matters such as estate planning, investments, domestic relations, or simple litigation. Some firms—known as boutiques—may handle more complex and sophisticated work. Law firms may define an area of practice and compete with larger firms for clients. Each small practice is bound to have its distinct personality and method of operation, but it is likely that a lawyer just starting out in a small firm will have a higher degree of visibility, will practice more as a generalist, and will more quickly take on additional responsibilities.

A solo practitioner practices entirely alone with only secretaries and legal assistants employed in the office. As soon as an associate comes on board, the practice is no longer solo. More and more, however, lawyers who might have been drawn to a solo practice are sharing space and equipment in order to keep costs down and have a more flexible time schedule. It would be beneficial, however, for the lawyer who chooses to be completely self-employed to acquire some sort of mentor or guide who can give the kind of counsel and instruction offered by the more senior members of a larger law firm.

■ *Government*

Government organizations that employ lawyers do not have the same kind of autonomy as do private employers. Often, management decisions in government—including budgetary issues—originate in a legislative body rather than at the headquarters. The kind of work a government lawyer does depends on the nature of the work done by a particular organization.

The Department of Justice and the Defense Department are two of the largest federal employers of lawyers. Beyond them, there are numerous agencies, boards, and commissions in the federal government that employ lawyers, including the Internal Revenue Service, National Aeronautics and Space Administration, Securities and Exchange Commission, Federal Reserve System, Federal Communications Commission, and Federal Trade Commission. Outside Washington, government lawyers may work in a U.S. Attorney's office, with local district attorneys, with a state attorney's office, as attorney for a municipality, or in one of many other federal regional offices.

The focus of legal activity for a state is in the office of the State Attorney General. The state regulatory departments of banking, insurance, securities, and public utilities all employ staff attorneys. The legislative branch of state government also employs lawyers to work on bill drafting, law revision, legislative review of administrative regulations, and so on. Some states use a centralized clearinghouse for hiring, such as the U.S. Civil Service Commission, but many states do not. You may have to research and persevere in order to traverse the complex bureaucracy of the numerous agencies that exist in all 50 states. An exploration of opportunities for state government employment will require your best organized effort.

Local government also offers many potential opportunities for work. Besides work related to criminal prosecution and defense, there is richly varied work on the civil side of local government, including such things as land use planning; utilities law in departments within city governments and in special districts, such as water, school, and regional planning; real property issues; and legislative counsel.

Finally, the military services represent one of the largest employers of law school graduates in the country. Although the military legal system differs from the civilian system, your law school preparation will serve you well if you choose this route. The salary, benefits, and security offered by the military make this avenue attractive to many graduates.

■ Business Organizations

There is a wide range of opportunities in business, though—as in
government—management decisions are frequently made outside
the legal department. The nature of the legal work depends on the
organization. If you join a corporate legal staff, you may eventually
head the law department of that organization, which may consist
of just a few lawyers or possibly more than 400. Lawyers in
corporations may handle interpretation of agreements,
negotiations, and preventive legal advice. Lawyers also handle
regulatory work in industries that are subject to government
regulation, such as utilities, transportation, communications, and
the food and drug industries. Corporations also retain attorneys to
work in their tax departments, or in research and development.
Some people choose this route because the pay and benefits are
good but the hours are more stable than in a large law firm.

■ Judicial Clerkships

Although clerkships may be classified as government work, they
can be considered a separate category because of the unique
opportunities offered and the limited duration of these jobs.
Clerkships offer new lawyers the opportunity to observe closely
the trial and appellate system, to work with experienced litigators,
and to strengthen one's writing skills. These positions are not
normally considered career paths but rather gateways that will lead
to future career options. Most judicial clerkships are only one or
two years long. There are generally far fewer clerkships available
than students who vie for these positions, and the quality of the
experience will usually correlate strongly to the personality and
values of the judge served.

■ Other Options

Besides the standard areas of private practice, government, business,
clerkships, and public interest, a certain number of law school
graduates each year will accept academic opportunities after several
years of practice or return to school for advanced studies. In addition,
there are new employer groups—such as foundations, hospitals, bar
associations, universities, and consulting firms—who have not
previously employed lawyers but are doing so in increasing numbers.

■ Nonlegal Careers

The phenomenon of lawyers in nonlegal positions grew out of the need of business and industry to have people with legal training in strategic positions, in order to troubleshoot—that is, to anticipate and solve little problems before they become big problems.

The authors of *Nonlegal Careers for Lawyers*[1] point out that certain skills learned in law school are basic to a variety of nonlegal positions, especially in the business world. These skills, specifically, are: 1) the ease in dealing with legal terminology and concepts, 2) ability to analyze facts, and 3) ability to persuade others. The book outlines various career possibilities in business organizations (such as real estate, public relations, insurance, and employee relations) and other organizations (education, health care, media, accounting, publishing, and so forth).

Summary

The profession of law is not a single, homogeneous profession; you should view it rather as a wide umbrella, encompassing the overlapping and still-developing fields within the practice of law. Law school, then, does not specifically train you as an expert in any particular kind of law, but rather acts as a springboard into various professional opportunities. It is up to you to make the most of the opportunities that come along, and to seek out opportunities for yourself.

For a more focused look at how law school trains lawyers, and what the experience of law school may be like for you, please turn to Chapter 3.

---

[1]Utley, Frances, with Gary A. Munneke, *Nonlegal Careers for Lawyers: In the Private Sector*. 2d edition. *Chicago: American Bar Association/Law Student Division, 1991.*

Chapter 3

The Experience of Law School: What You Can Expect

The skills and behavior that made you successful during your four years of college will not necessarily work for you in law school, at least not in quite the same way. The methods of teaching, the professors themselves, the types of students, and even the goal of the educational process will all require your best adaptive skills. The study of law encourages you to look at all sides of a question, and when you think you have an answer, to be prepared to ask yet another question. You will be asked to explore not whether the answer is *a* or *b*, but what the consequences are if *a* happens, and/or if *b* happens. In addition, you may be asked to understand and argue the opposite side of the answer you believe to be true. Learning how to advocate a particular point of view within the legal system and simultaneously balancing an opposite point of view can be disconcerting when you first begin your studies in law school.

In high school, you may have become accustomed to continual monitoring of your progress, sometimes in the form of a weekly quiz. In college, this kind of scholastic babysitting decreases somewhat, but many college courses still rely on midterms and papers as well as final exams. Most courses in the first year of law school have exams only at the end of the semester. Moreover, these exams will not ask you to regurgitate the professor's lecture but to apply what was discussed in class. The facts or hypothetical situations given on the exam may not even remotely resemble the material you examined in class.

The lack of regular monitoring may lead you to feel uncertain of whether you are understanding the material as you should, and students will often form study groups with classmates to compare their understanding. This can lead to a sense of camaraderie or a sense of competition, sometimes both. The most important thing to remember is that **you must keep up with your studies.** Reading and studying should be a daily activity.

The First Year of Law School

It might be useful to think about law school as two distinct parts: The first year, and the rest of it.

There is no question that the first year of law school is especially demanding and difficult; it is often exciting as well. You may have heard about the Socratic approach to teaching. Many law professors use some variation on this method for their first-year classes, though the pedagogic methods of the law school faculty can vary with each individual teacher. With the Socratic method, the professor's role is to pose questions, and the students learn from one another's responses. Questions relate to the assigned material, which consists primarily of appellate court decisions, usually contained in a casebook in which the author has compiled a number of decisions. You will be expected to read cases which you will analyze and dissect in class. It is crucial that you do not fall behind; once you do, it may be extremely difficult to catch up. Your first assignment will typically be posted before your first class session. You will be assigned to write a "brief," or a synopsis of the case, to aid in your recitation and understanding. You may be asked to state the facts about the case and its decision, perhaps some procedural history of the case as it worked its way from the trial court into the court whose decision you have read. If you ask a question, the professor is likely to answer with another question posed to you. A value is placed on logic and the capacity to read material accurately, and then to *look beyond your first response to a problem* to analyze all of its implications, including the strengths and weaknesses of the options available and the future consequences of present decisions. This is part of the process of thinking like a lawyer, being able to perceive not just the black and white of life, but the vast areas of gray.

Professorial styles vary: some professors will ask you to stand, some will expect you to sit. Some will be more formal or informal, some courteous, some abrupt or intimidating. You should not expect these sessions to teach you information the same way an undergraduate lecture does. The expectation is not simply that you will learn a rule, but that you will learn how rules evolve; you will also expand your analytical powers and become accustomed to oral presentation.

■ *Required Courses*

In the first year, courses are usually all required. They are fairly standard and may include civil procedure, constitutional law, contracts, torts, criminal law, property law, and legal research and writing. These subject areas form the foundation for the upper-level electives and they provide the concepts essential to an understanding of our legal system. It is important to note that, while first-year curricula at all schools share a great deal in common, there is growing innovation and variety within first-year programs. You should examine law school bulletins carefully to see whether and how a school has modernized its curriculum. A brief description of the basic required courses is included below.

Procedure (usually *Civil Procedure*). Procedure is the study of the processes of litigation and dispute resolution in the United States—that is, how lawyers bring a problem from the outside world into the world of the courts. (Civil cases are those in which no criminal penalties are sought.) The topics covered in a procedure course are how lawsuits are started and ended, what powers the decision makers have, and what the structure of courts is and has been. Increasingly, civil courses are devoting some attention to methods of alternative dispute resolution.

Contracts. The contract—an agreement between persons that can be enforced in court—appears in every area of law. The study of contract law provides one of the best vehicles for teaching a wide range of essential legal skills and concepts. This course is, therefore, basic and you can expect to continually refer to the material you learn throughout your years as a lawyer, no matter what kind of law you practice. The class usually covers such topics as who can make an enforceable contract, what rules must be complied with for a contract to be enforceable in the court, how the obligations created by a contract arise and are then discharged, what defenses exist in lawsuits that are based on contracts, and remedies.

Torts. A tort is a wrong for which the law provides a civil penalty (as opposed to a criminal one) and which is not a breach of contract. Examples might be a car accident, a plane crash, a fall on an icy sidewalk, careless surgery, and so forth. This course is likely to delve into intentional torts, such as assault and battery, false imprisonment, trespass, infliction of emotional distress, and invasion of privacy. A good deal of your study of torts will revolve around negligence cases—that is, when the law imposes a liability because of carelessness (as opposed to purposeful conduct). You may also study product liability, a body of law designed to protect injured consumers, as well as defamation, invasion of privacy, and the like.

Property. This class begins with a discussion of the origins of Anglo-American property law and deals with a wide variety of concepts, including the possession of land and objects; the types of rights (or "interests") one can have in property; the legal nature of the landlord-tenant relationship; the methods by which one can transfer property and protect the parties' interests in the process; and the public and private regulation of land use.

Criminal Law. This course teaches such things as the elements to be proved by the prosecuting attorney in order to allow a jury to find a person guilty of a crime, defenses, constitutional requirements for protecting the rights of the accused, and other miscellany of criminal law. You will study such issues as the right to trial by jury, double jeopardy, the state's burden of proof, and conspiracy.

Constitutional Law. The constitutional law course is the study of the essential governmental framework, and the basic rights of individuals in this country. These legal concepts are taught through decisions of the United States Supreme Court, the final arbiter of constitutional issues. You will learn such things as the Supreme Court's authority to declare congressional acts unconstitutional, the legal relationships between the state and federal government and among the branches of the federal government, the powers exercised by the federal government, and the protection offered to individuals. You may also study the mechanics of Supreme Court practice.

Legal Research and Writing. Students should come to law school with basic writing skills. Building on those skills, Legal Research and Writing will teach you how to research legal issues; how to prepare documents such as a memorandum (a written response to a legal question) and a brief (an argument to the appellate court setting forth the reasons you feel a decision was wrong, or right, depending on which side you're on); what types of legal books and journals exist, how to use them and where to find them; and how to use computers and legal publishing services. It will familiarize you with the law library, which is likely to be your second home while you're in law school. Another component of this course frequently is the oral argument. In this exercise, also called moot court, you are given a particular set of facts and assigned to represent a party in the fictional case. You will need to do extensive research and produce a formal legal brief; at the end of the year, you will argue your case in front of three "judges"—professors, practicing lawyers, or senior members of the class.

The Second and Third Years of Law School

Once you finish your first year, the intensity level often drops dramatically. You are permitted to pick from a wide array of courses. You may begin to think a great deal more about jobs; you may work part-time for a law firm and begin to think about life after law school. There may be a tendency for classroom participation to drop off a bit, as students pursue part-time jobs, law-related activities, and other interests. But it is important to remember that the classroom experience continues to be a crucial aspect of your law school education. Outside activity should supplement, rather than replace, classroom learning.

■ *Choosing Electives*

Among the courses you may choose from in the second and third years of law school are the following samples, culled from a random look at various law school catalogs: administrative law, antitrust law, asylum and refugee law, commercial law, copyrights, corporate finance, employment discrimination, environmental law, estate and gift taxes, evidence, family law, federal income tax, hazardous substance litigation, insurance, international law, labor law, law of the sea, ocean and coastal law, public land law, and securities regulation. Pedagogy in upper-level courses is more varied than that of the first-year courses; the curriculum is often designed to include problem solving and research projects as well as lecture-style teaching. Almost all law schools have an upper-level writing requirement which requires in-depth work on a particular topic or some other kind of expository writing.

Other Aspects of Life in Law School

■ *Clinical Courses*

A majority of schools offer students the opportunity for authentic experiences as lawyers by involving them with clients. Some schools run their own clinics (often geared toward indigent populations); other schools offer credit for students' work in an agency off campus. Some schools involve students in simulations of actual legal situations. Law school educators continue to debate the merits of various practice-related activities offered by law schools and their relationship to law study. Many clinical programs are still developing, so quality varies from school to school. (For additional discussion of clinical courses, see Chapter 6.)

■ *Law Reviews and Other Scholarly Activities*

The law review is a scholarly journal published at most law schools four to six times a year for lawyers, judges, and professors. Articles are contributed by legal scholars, law professors, practitioners, and students. The law review is published by students under the guidance of a professor-advisor, and an invitation to work on the law review is generally based on academic performance and/or a writing competition. A number of schools have one or more specialized law reviews as well.

If you become a member of the law review, your editorial responsibilities will include proofreading the text of submitted articles, checking the legal citations for content and accuracy, and ascertaining that the form and style of all articles conform to standard law review style. Additionally, you will be expected to write an article for publication in the journal. Although this is essentially an extracurricular activity, the work can take up an extraordinary amount of your time. It is an excellent introduction to the kind of disciplined work that attorneys do.

Besides the law review, there are other opportunities to engage in scholarly writing. Upper-division seminars and legal essay contests all provide venues in which to showcase your writing abilities.

Most schools have special-interest groups focusing on specific areas of the law you may want to explore. These groups are often a good way to find your particular niche in the field of law, and they may expand your list of contacts as well. Some of these groups include the student bar association, legal philosophy discussion groups, lecture-organizing committee, law school newspaper, international law society, environmental or urban law association, various volunteer groups, and associations of minority-group students.

Chapter 4

Gaining Admission to Law School:
Preparation and Self-assessment

Depending on where you are on the continuum—whether you're precollege or beyond college—there are some aspects of your law school preparation that are within your control and some that are not. It's too late now to improve your grades if they're not as high as you would like, but you **can** evaluate your other credentials and get a realistic picture of your stronger and weaker points. Such self-assessment will be invaluable when you begin to gather information about law schools to decide where to apply (see Chapters 5 and 6).

The two most important factors that will determine your admission to law school are undeniably your undergraduate grades and your score on the Law School Admission Test. Nevertheless, you should bear in mind that other factors—namely, the undergraduate school you attended, your letters of recommendation and personal statement (part of your application), and certain aspects of your life experience, particularly if you can make it come alive in writing—will all be used to evaluate you as a candidate for admission.

Distinguishing yourself in any one area is by no means a guarantee of admission to law school, but neither is a less-than-exemplary grade-point average or LSAT score necessarily a deterrent to your acceptance. Each applicant will be considered on his or her own merits. All other things being equal, a school's wish to have a geographically balanced or culturally diverse student population can sometimes influence a decision. Therefore, when assessing your own chances, consider each component separately before giving any one undue weight. Meanwhile, take all the necessary steps to optimize your credentials in each area where you are still able to make a difference.

In this chapter we discuss some of the various elements in your prelaw self-evaluation, including both academic and nonacademic factors: your college years, the Law School Admission Test, and a variety of additional ingredients in your personal life. In later chapters, we discuss in more practical detail how all this material is conveyed to and assessed by the law schools, including suggestions on securing letters of recommendation and preparing a personal statement for your application package. For now, let us examine the most important components of your prelaw self-evaluation and explore ways you might make the most of the picture as it emerges.

Prelaw Preparation: Choosing a College

If you are still at the stage of selecting an undergraduate school—and you have law in the back of your mind—you will want to enroll in a college or university that is able to stand on its own merits as an institution that will demand the best of you and prepare you for a competitive and complex world. You will want to demonstrate to law school admission committees later that your college years have challenged your thinking and sharpened your analytical skills. When gathering information about undergraduate colleges to attend, you may also want to consider schools whose graduates have respectable law school admission records and law school performances. Find out if the college has a prelaw advisor on its staff. It's to your advantage to attend an undergraduate school that does employ someone who is professionally experienced in counseling students who are considering law school.

College catalogs or admission personnel may provide information on the reputation of various departments within the college (especially if you have a particular major in mind), the number of Ph.D.s on the faculty, and the overall reputation of the school in the academic community. When seeking information of this kind, it's wise to gather information from additional sources besides the school itself, since most schools naturally want to promote themselves as positively as possible.

Your grade-point average and your LSAT score will certainly be weighed more heavily than the reputation of your alma mater. Nevertheless, in some cases when an admission committee must choose among candidates with similar credentials, the quality of the college you attended may shed some light on the relative value of your GPA. Law school admission committees are informed about who has applied to their school from particular institutions, what the decision was, and what the accepted student's progress was once he or she enrolled. You should, therefore, be equally informed; the prelaw advisor on campus may be able to provide you with some of this information.

Once you have selected an undergraduate school, introduce yourself to a prelaw advisor as soon as possible. The advisor can guide you in your course selection and can help you prepare for law school at every stage, up to and including guiding you through the application process itself. You may also want to explore whether the college you are considering sponsors a prelaw club:

such a club can serve as a valuable vehicle for information about the legal profession and as a focal point for law school admission officers, practicing lawyers, and others who may come to the campus to share information. This will become especially important when you begin to think more actively about choosing law schools to which you will apply.

Making the Most of Your Undergraduate Education

There is no prelaw curriculum of required courses that corresponds to the premed courses a student must take before being admitted to medical school. On the contrary, you should be very wary of courses that purport to be introductory law or the "law and" courses (Law and Society, Law and Business); while they may be interesting, and possibly even have value in aiding your decision about **whether** the field of law interests you, they are in no way related to, or relevant to, the training you will receive in law school. Law schools prefer that you reserve your legal study for law school.

■ *Course Selection*

Most law school admission personnel look beyond the raw number represented by your undergraduate grade-point average to evaluate the rigor and depth of the courses you selected. They are looking for evidence that you can master the basic skills required of a lawyer. Foremost among these skills is the ability to write clearly, reason logically, and analyze creatively. An undergraduate career that is narrow, unchallenging, or vocationally oriented is not the best preparation for law school. If you stick with a basic liberal arts curriculum, you will be headed in the right direction. According to the Law School Admission Council's *Statement of Good Admission Practices*:

> It is proper to prefer students who have taken courses such as those that develop skills in both written and oral communications, develop analytical and problem-solving skills, or promote familiarity with the humanities and social sciences to understand the human condition and the social context in which legal problems arise.

The range of acceptable majors is broad. Almost any course of study that engenders mental discipline and intellectual curiosity can lay the foundation for a successful legal education and professional career.

Thomas L. Pearce, a prelaw advisor at the University of Virginia in Charlottesville, advises his students in this manner: "Read, read, read more than you think you can. ... Getting used to language as the coin of your realm is really smart. A course or two in economics or accounting [will give you] some familiarity with the way money moves through society. ..." Pearce also recommends "a course in public speaking; a course in logic—but calculus is just as good,"—and finally—"something with computers—do not ignore the word processor, because you'll be pounding one in law school."

English language and literature courses are indispensable to every aspiring law student; courses in journalism are useful as well, particularly in training students to write clearly and succinctly. History is worthwhile, too, especially American history; political science relates strongly to the law, government, and politics. Philosophy courses are useful because they demand the same kind of rigorous, logical thinking as does the law. Natural science courses test your ability to analyze diverse and complex information and to arrive at creative solutions and conclusions. Engineering courses, too, have value to the extent that they prepare students for in-depth analysis, but a technical education must be balanced with liberal arts courses for breadth of study.

- *Major Course of Study*

Listed below are 10 subjects that law school applicants most commonly declare as their undergraduate majors. Although the percentages apply to the 99,000 law school applicants for 1990-91, the order of the subjects themselves has not changed significantly since the early 1980s. There does appear to be a bit more emphasis on business, economics, and finance in recent years.

- Political Science (17.8 percent)
- Arts and Humanities (12.3 percent)
- Social Sciences/Help Professions (10.1 percent)
- Business/Management (8.3 percent)
- History (6.9 percent)
- English (6.9 percent)

- Economics (6.0 percent)
- Psychology (4.7 percent)
- All Natural Sciences (4.3 percent)
- Finance (4.1 percent)
- Psychology (4.7 percent)

Important: Do not infer from this information that any one specific major guarantees more success than any other major in being accepted to law school. Rather, these statistics show that the most commonly chosen major fields of study emphasize skills that are useful in the study and practice of law. Indeed, some law schools will select students from less common majors just to assure a diverse student body.

Neither should you infer that any particular course of study will be more helpful to you later in law school. Although English and history majors have the opportunity to develop writing skills through their term paper assignments, engineering and chemistry majors are more accustomed to problem solving and recitation, a standard part of first-year law school. In fact, science students are often more schooled in analysis and logic than are students in liberal arts. Rather than looking for the perfect major, or courses that will serve you well in law school, you are better off looking for excellent teachers who will contribute to your overall education and enhance your skills as a thinker.

■ *Transcript Evaluation*

Many law schools consider trends in your transcript along with your numerical average. Thus, the student who started out with average grades and later performed exceptionally may be favored over the student who started out with excellent grades and then faltered after a time. In a similar scenario, every year there are a number of students who at one time flunked out of college but later returned and did well. Says one admission-file reader at a highly competitive law school: "We accept some individuals who either came back from military service 'reborn' or who, for a variety of other reasons, settled down and did strong academic work. We will readily work with someone who finishes strong despite a poor beginning."

If you are among the "reborn," be sure to offer some tangible evidence of your improvement. You're not likely to impress a law school committee merely by presenting a letter that proclaims you have suddenly found yourself.

In addition, a student who manages to earn a high grade-point average through easy, nondemanding courses will not fool law school admission staff. Such a transcript is not an accurate record of a student's capabilities: this student probably has not developed good study habits, critical reading and thinking skills, or a coherent writing style.

Along the same lines, be wary of pass-fail courses; keep them to a minimum. Admission-file readers usually find them an obstacle to accurate measurement of a student's achievement, and they suspect that a student may have put little effort into such classes. Some colleges do not offer grades for all or part of their undergraduate coursework, although they may instead provide comprehensive narrative transcripts. One way to supplement information relating to a "pass" grade you may have earned is to provide written support from the faculty member who taught the course.

Another question that sometimes arises is whether graduate work will strengthen your credentials and increase your chances of acceptance at a law school. Generally speaking, law school admission personnel are more interested in your academic accomplishments as an undergraduate. Grades have a different value in graduate school, since most graduate students usually get "A"s and "B"s. Law schools do not combine your undergraduate GPA with that of your graduate record. However, your successful completion of a graduate program may be another element that works in your favor, especially if it was a demanding program—for example, a Ph.D. in physics—or if your graduate study took place at a competitive institution and you can demonstrate a dedication to your studies.

■ Other Things to Keep in Mind

As you proceed in your college career, taking rigorous courses and getting good grades, you will also benefit by developing good personal relationships with some of your teachers, especially those who stimulate you intellectually and who are in a position to observe your best work. Eventually, you will want to ask for letters of recommendation (see Chapter 7) and you would be wise to lay the foundation for these requests early on. You will probably have an academic advisor; if you have any input as to who your advisor will be, try to select someone who has knowledge of, and an interest in, law school admission. The ideal advisor is someone who has a track record of writing recommendations for students who go on to law school.

As we mentioned earlier, register with a prelaw advisor, attend a prelaw orientation if one is offered, and stay alert for any other prelaw-related activities on or off campus.

Review your grade pattern and performance record periodically, taking corrective steps if necessary to improve any low standings. Read as much as you can, above and beyond your required reading if possible.

The Law School Admission Test (LSAT)

■ *The Score and Its Relationship to Admission*

All schools presently approved by the American Bar Association (ABA) or the Federation of Law Societies of Canada (FLSC) require you to take the LSAT as part of the admission process. (On rare occasions, an exception may be made for people with certain disabilities.) Your LSAT score, while not the only deciding factor in admission to law school, is nevertheless a critical factor in the initial sorting of hundreds of applications submitted to a law school admission office. A low LSAT score will not necessarily block admission to law school, although it may block admission to the more selective schools. By the same token, a high LSAT score alone will not guarantee your admission to a particular law school, but it will allow you to consider a broader range of schools, particularly those that are more competitive. Individual law schools set their own standards, and when you begin to gather information about law schools, you can find out the acceptable range. Keep in mind that other factors—discussed in this chapter—can help compensate for a weaker score just as some factors can—though less often—detract from a strong score.

■ *What the Test Measures*

The LSAT is designed to measure skills that are considered essential for success in law school. It does not measure any common body of knowledge or specific discipline. There is no set of facts or theories to study, although there **are** ways to prepare for the test (discussed below). Rather, the LSAT tests such things as:

the reading and comprehension of complex texts with accuracy and insight, the organization and management of information and the ability to draw reasonable inferences from it, the ability to reason critically, and the analysis and evaluation of the reasoning and argument of others.

The test itself consists of five 35-minute sections of multiple choice questions in three different item types. A 30-minute writing sample is administered at the end of the test. Copies of the writing sample are sent to all the law schools to which you apply. For a more detailed description of the various sections of the test, consult the *LSAT/LSDAS Registration and Information Book*, available from Law Services, law schools, undergraduate schools, and other locations.

■ *Preparing for the LSAT*

The most important thing to understand about taking the LSAT was perhaps expressed most succinctly by prelaw advisor Margot Baker: "You don't just ... show up one day and take it." Baker stresses most emphatically, as do virtually all prelaw advisors, "you need to prepare for the LSAT." But because the LSAT is not an achievement test, and does not test a body of knowledge, there is a limit to what any form of preparation can do. So how do you prepare?

Effective test preparation should concentrate on three things: One, it should familiarize you with how the test looks, its sections and formats, the mechanics of taking the test, and the timing you can expect. In short, you want to assure that there will be no logistical or procedural surprises on the day you take the LSAT. The *LSAT/LSDAS Registration and Information Book* discusses in greater detail what you can expect on the day of the test.

Second, a good preparation program will teach certain test-taking strategies that will both save time and increase your scoring potential. For example, there is no penalty for wrong answers; therefore, you should always guess, after eliminating answers you believe to be incorrect. Also, you should pace yourself; if you are spending too much time on a difficult question, move on. Because specific knowledge is not being tested, you should never answer a question based on your own knowledge or experience, nor should you read more into a problem than is on the page. Additional test-taking strategies are outlined in the *LSAT/LSDAS Registration and Information Book*, and in the test preparation materials published by Law Services.

Finally, a good preparation program will teach and reinforce the analytical and logical skills necessary for success on the exam. The best way to achieve this particular goal is to practice. Many students have found it useful to practice with sample questions from the disclosed tests published by Law Services: *Official LSAT PrepTests* allow you to practice by taking disclosed tests under simulated (timed) conditions, so that you may familiarize yourself thoroughly with test directions, test mechanics, and question types. You can obtain a free sample LSAT at any law school or *LSAT/LSDAS Registration and Information Book* distribution point. Other test preparation materials offered by Law Services, such as the *Official LSAT Prepkit*, are listed in the *Registration and Information Book* as well.

There are commercial test preparation courses, although Law Services does not endorse or sponsor them, nor do these courses represent Law Services. All students should exercise care in selecting such courses, especially with regard to the accuracy of information these courses provide regarding the LSAT and any other law school admission policies. Complete and updated information regarding the LSAT is made available each year in the *Registration and Information Book*. Students should also be skeptical of any extravagant claims made about a preparation course's ability to raise a student's score.

You should approach the LSAT seriously and realistically, without panic or undue anxiety. A certain degree of tension is normal, and simply signifies that your mental adrenalin is functioning. But you must keep your anxiety level under control so that it does not impair your performance on the test. The key to success is preparing responsibly and then concentrating on the test itself.

■ When to Take the Test

The LSAT is administered four times a year, usually in June, October, December, and February. You should plan on taking either the June or October test in the year **preceding** your expected admission to law school. If you're planning to attend law school directly after college, the June test would take place at the end of your junior year; the October test would take place in the fall of your senior year.

There are several reasons for taking the test earlier rather than later. The deadline for many law school applications is in February, and it is advantageous—though not necessary—to know your score before you mail out your applications. Knowing your score will help you identify the law schools most likely to admit you. If you take the test even earlier—in June—you will have the opportunity to retake the test if a problem should arise (see next section). You should certainly take the test by the December preceding the year you wish to enroll at the very latest. If you intend to attend law school directly after college, this would be December in your senior year. February scores will not reach law schools in time to meet most application deadlines, but some schools will wait for late scores in special cases.

■ *Retaking the LSAT*

Under normal circumstances, a student should plan on taking the LSAT only one time. For most students, retaking the test does **not** result in a significant increase in the score. If, however, you feel that your current score does not truly reflect your capabilities, you may want to take the test again, especially if there were special circumstances—such as illness—that are relevant to the poor score. You should also let the law schools know about any extenuating circumstances, providing documentation, if possible. Understand, however, that most law schools will average your scores—unless the disparity is great, in which case the admission office is likely to review your entire file for an explanation.

Any test score on your record during the five years prior to your application will be sent automatically—along with your current score—to the schools to which you apply, You may also request (in writing) that scores from as far back as 10 years be sent, but it is best to inquire of individual schools whether sending those scores will have any value in the admission process.

(See Chapter 7 for more about the Law School Data Assembly Service [LSDAS] and the mechanics of applying to law school in general).

The *Registration and Information Book* provides additional information about test registration (including changes in your test date or test center, alternative dates for Sabbath observers, accommodations for test takers with disabilities, and other information on the scoring of the LSAT).

Preparing to Return to School After an Absence

As we mentioned earlier in the book, there are those students who go to law school right after they graduate from college, and there are those who—entertaining some last-minute uncertainties—delay law school for a year, or several, until they've clarified their goals satisfactorily. There are also those who choose law school later in life, as a career or life change, or for other personal reasons such as wanting some work experience prior to law study. (See Table 4.1 below for information on the average age of applicants in recent years.) The amount of time that elapses between college graduation and application to law school can affect how admission personnel regard a candidate's admission.

Joseph Burns, prelaw advisor at Boston College observes, "If they're out longer than five, six, or ten years, law schools do look at them differently, they do (look at) their most recent work—whether it's graduate academic work or employment—and weigh that more heavily. Simultaneously, they (may) discount *to some degree* the GPA, *but that makes the LSAT more important.*" [emphasis added]

Table 4.1
Applicant Volumes by Age

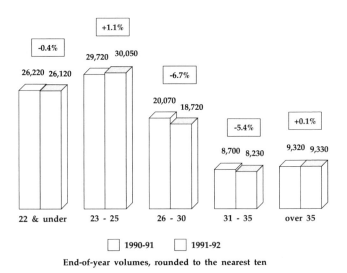

End-of-year volumes, rounded to the nearest ten

Some potential applicants—particularly those who have been out of school for some time—may find it helpful to go back and take even one class, just to get back into the academic environment, to remember how it feels to be treated as a student ("It can be tough on your ego sometimes," Burns points out), and to get used to studying and writing again.

For those of you whose professional positions entail a good deal of reading and writing, especially if it involves analysis, problem solving, and so forth—you will want to highlight these aspects of your work in your personal statement; you will want employers whom you ask for letters of recommendation to emphasize these strengths as well.

Additional Factors That May Affect Admission

A poor GPA or weak LSAT will make law school admission difficult but not impossible. Other criteria are taken into consideration as well, and—particularly if your letters of recommendation are strong, and you can articulately state your case for admission in your personal statement— factors such as the ones listed below will be considered as part of your education by admission personnel. Law schools do want to make a sincere effort to evaluate you as a person, not just as a collection of numbers; however, it is up to you to supply the information that will help the law schools learn who you are and what outstanding characteristics make you special. In Chapter 7, we discuss the importance of letters of recommendation and your personal statement in rounding out the picture of you as a law school applicant. Below are several categories of information you may want to keep in mind while assessing your own chances of admission. If a particular category applies to you, be sure to expand upon it in your personal statement (see Chapter 7) which you will submit with your law school application.

- *Extracurricular Activities and Community Activities*

Merely having your name associated with a particular group or association will not gain you any special recognition, since most students do take part to some degree in extracurricular activities. However, it is your active participation and demonstrated leadership abilities that will put you in a more favorable light. If you have not been in college recently, community activities will serve a similar purpose in rounding out the picture of you that emerges on your application.

These need not be law-related activities: you may have been active in student government, political groups, an honors organization, magazine or newspaper work, sports competition, the debate team, volunteer work for a community agency, PTA, fundraising for a charitable institution, and the like. What is important here is that you are able to cite examples of how these activities employed your ability to work with others, or how these endeavors relate to the basic skills of lawyering, such as writing, analyzing, decision making, and so forth. Quality is more important than quantity; a list of organizations and activities on your application with no attendant explanation that evaluates the experience has no meaning to an admission-file reader. Remember to state, then evaluate.

There is one other caveat, however. In discussing the relative importance of community and extracurricular activities for undergraduate students, prelaw advisor Thomas Pearce advises students to "dive in, but **never** at the peril of (your) grades." All the well-meaning activity in the world will not do you any good if you cannot keep up with your academic work, so do not let your grades slip because you don't have time to study. No admission officer at any law school will overlook poor or slipping grades based on this excuse.

■ *Work Experience*

Referring to your employment experience can be very important, particularly if you have been out of school for some time. Be sure to cite specific examples of achievement that relate directly to the experience of lawyering such as writing, analyzing, decision making, and leadership. Your task is not to highlight the job, but to demonstrate how you have excelled at it.

■ *Minority Status*

Law schools are instructed in the *Statement of Good Admission Practices,* set forth by the Law School Admission Council, to

> give special consideration to applicants who are members of cultural, ethnic, or racial groups that have not had adequate opportunities to develop and

demonstrate potential for academic achievement and would not otherwise be meaningfully represented in the entering class.

Specifically, most ABA-approved law schools do have recruitment programs that actively seek qualified African-American, Hispanic, Asian, and American Indian students and other students of color. Additionally, many schools consider such factors as economic and educational disadvantage when considering a candidate for admission.

This endeavor has wide-ranging benefits for students and for the profession as a whole. Among the benefits are increased diversity in law school as well as in the legal profession, and a growth in the number of legally trained professionals to serve an increasingly diverse society. Accordingly, it is to your advantage to note on your application any relevant information concerning your ethnic, cultural, or racial background, or any aspect of your life that may contribute to a diverse student body.

For more comprehensive information on this subject, consult *Thinking About Law School: A Minority Guide*, published by Law Services.

■ *Military Service*

Some schools weigh military service and achievement more heavily than others. If you are a veteran, consider how your military record has enhanced your potential as a prospective law student. Focus on key themes such as discipline, leadership, and tenacity. Use your personal statement (see Chapter 7) as an opportunity to bring these issues to light.

■ *Parents and Relatives*

If you are a relative of an alumnus, you may be given special consideration by admission personnel at some schools—provided you already have met the school's basic admission requirements. As one law school dean admits, "I don't think it's in the interest of the law school to go out of our way to make enemies of alumni ... There may be an institutional interest that is served by admitting that applicant: good will and good alumni relations might be served ...

However, [the institutional interest factor] is definitely not going to get any applicant up over the line who isn't in the admission range already." Some schools have strict policies against this.

Summary

If you've done all that you can to prepare yourself for law school up to this point, and you've realistically assessed your own credentials so that you can build your strongest case, you are ready to take a look at the schools themselves. Your goal is to find those schools that will meet your individual needs, and to the extent that you are thoughtful and realistic in your choices (which does **not** preclude aiming high as well; see Chapter 7), you will still be involved in the self-assessment process to some extent.

In the next chapter, we discuss how you can best gather the information you need to evaluate the various schools you might attend, and what the important elements are in assessing a school.

Chapter 5

Gathering Information About Law Schools

Finding the right law school is a challenge. Be prepared to put as much time and energy and resourcefulness into your research as possible, so that you can find the school or schools that is the best match for you. There are many different criteria by which you can assess a law school, not the least of which is whether it is likely to accept you as a student. Your LSAT score and your grade-point average will influence your admissability to a large degree, along with the criteria discussed in Chapter 4. However, you should begin by assembling a list of schools that interest you, based on some of the factors discussed in this chapter. You may wish to refer to *The Official Guide to U.S. Law Schools,* published annually by Law School Admission Services. Then you can examine these schools more carefully in terms of your own admission possibilities. In Chapter 7, we discuss how you can use the admission profile grids contained in the *Official Guide* to assess your chances of admission to a particular school. You may have to revise your list of law school choices on the basis of your further exploration. This process will help you match your credentials to schools that appeal to you. You should not apply to any school that you do not want to attend, and do not plan to attend.

However, your evaluation of a law school is only as good as the information that you collect. Statistics, as well as specific programs for particular schools, may vary from year to year, and some information may be more or less subjective, depending on the source. Getting the facts requires patience and determination. You are likely to hear conflicting reports about the same school; you may get pressure from family and friends about which school to attend; your financial situation may lead you to believe that you cannot apply to the school that appeals to you. Chapter 8 discusses financial aid in more detail.

In this chapter, we first survey and evaluate the various sources from which you may gather information about law schools. Next, we discuss the elements you may want to consider when taking a school's measure for your own best fit. You should be as careful selecting a law school as you were in evaluating your decision to investigate law as a career.

- **The Official Guide to U.S. Law Schools**

This comprehensive guide, compiled and published by Law School Admission Services in cooperation with the American Bar Association and the Association of American Law Schools, provides summary profiles of all ABA-approved law schools in both narrative and tabular format, arranged both alphabetically and geographically by state. All statistics are updated annually by the law schools themselves, and most schools provide statistical grids that show admission patterns for the previous year based on GPA and LSAT scores. The *Official Guide* provides information on enrollment and student body, faculty, library and physical facilities, admission, expenses, and a range of other items, including a chart titled "Key Facts for Minority Law School Applicants." Each entry also tells you where to write or call for further information about individual schools. (If you are interested in applying to Canadian schools, consult the *LSAT Registration and Information Book—Canadian Edition*, which contains similar information.) The Official Guide is available at Law School Forums (see page 48), from Law Services, and directly from some bookstores. For more information, phone 215.968.1001.

Other Publications

A variety of law school directories may be available in bookstores and libraries; you will have to use your own judgment as to the quality and reliability of the various publications you find. You are well advised to exercise skepticism about books that attempt to rank schools. Some criteria for personalized assessment are simply unquantifiable; and much information changes from year to year, and over time. There is also a certain amount of debate over what criteria should be used to assess schools. It is best to contact law schools directly for up-to-date information, and evaluate with your own personal profile in mind.

Your Undergraduate College: The Prelaw Advisor

If you attended or are presently enrolled in a college that employs a prelaw advisor, you have an important resource at your fingertips. Those of you who entered college with law on your mind probably know this, but those of you just beginning to consider law may not be aware of who and what a prelaw advisor is.

Prelaw advisors can guide you throughout the law school admission process, and they can be helpful in providing information about particular law schools. They can identify law schools that have accepted alumni from your college or university with academic profiles similar to your own (though you should certainly not narrow your focus only to those schools). They also are likely to be quite knowledgeable about law schools in your region. You should not expect a prelaw advisor to be informed about every program at every law school. It is also not a prelaw advisor's job to tell you where you should go to law school, but rather to offer suggestions based on your self-assessment. As we discussed in Chapter 4, the prelaw advisor may be adept at getting you started with your self-assessment if you haven't already begun the process. Nevertheless, the real research work about particular law schools is still up to you.

Prelaw advisors may also be able to advise you about special events in your area where you may have an opportunity to speak with law school representatives and lawyers themselves.

If you are already an alumnus of your school and beginning to consider a career change, don't be shy about contacting the prelaw advisor at your alma mater. If you no longer live in close proximity to your undergraduate college, you may wish to contact the prelaw advisor at any college or university in your area. Although their first obligation is to the students at their institution, many prelaw advisors say they welcome phone calls from any person seriously considering law school, and will be happy to offer their services if time permits.

The Law Schools

Naturally, for detailed information about a specific school, there is no better source than the law school itself. At your request, the admission office will mail you law school catalogs as well as brochures about any special opportunities and programs. Most law school admission staff are happy to answer your questions about admission requirements or faculty and student-body profiles. A school may even be willing to give you an idea of your chances of admission based on a summary of your credentials, although some may be reluctant to speculate about such matters over the phone. In addition to catalogs and brochures, a number of schools make available videocassettes that show you as well as tell you about the law school program.

Site visits. You should definitely try to visit a law school, especially if a school is one of several that are at the top of your list. A site visit gives you the feel of the campus, and can help you determine if you will be comfortable there. You can inspect the educational, professional, and recreational resources of both the school and the surrounding community. Additionally, being on campus gives you opportunities to talk personally with law school representatives, students, faculty, and members of various student associations.

"Many schools have open-house weekends, or special programs, or at least they will arrange a ... tour for the visitor," says Robert Gibson, prelaw advisor at the State University of New York, Albany. "[You might] start with a formal program, [but then] you end up drinking coffee wherever law students drink coffee. ... Be sure you talk to a couple of people who are first-year students, and you absolutely must contrast that by talking to students who are [in their] second or third year."

Gibson offers a suggestion for the student who cannot make such a visit. "If it's impossible to visit," he says, "there are other ways that the student can get that personal feeling about a law school. If it's a school that has a number of students from your own undergraduate school, call the [law school] admission office, get a name or two of current students who went to your school, contact them by phone." Gibson contends that in sharing an alma mater, "you have an entry"; in addition, "you have a basis for comparison in discussing that student's experience in light of his or her undergraduate experience."

Finally, Gibson reminds students that law schools often are willing to put interested students in touch with alumni in their area.

Law Forums, Law Fairs, and Other Special Events

The Law School Forums, organized by the Law School Admission Council, offer students the opportunity to meet and talk with law school representatives from around the United States in one central, urban location, usually a hotel meeting room. In 1992, 151 of the 176 ABA-approved law schools participated in one or more forums. At the forums, you can meet admission personnel, obtain admission materials, catalogs, and financial aid information; talk to Law Services representatives and purchase Law Services publications; learn about the mechanics of the application process; and view video programs that discuss issues related to attending law school. Each forum also holds information sessions for minority prospective students on application policies and procedures, law student life, and legal practice from a minority perspective. Forums are held in Atlanta, Boston, Chicago, Los Angeles, New York City, and Houston. Since few prospective applicants have the resources to visit all the schools that interest them, the Law School Forums offer an excellent alternative for information gathering and for making school contacts. Admission to the forums is free and open to anyone interested in learning about law school: high school students, college freshman, sophomores, juniors, seniors, and those who have already graduated from college. In Canada, a similar program called Law Fair is held twice a year in Toronto; information is available from any of the Canadian law schools.

Graduate/professional school days. Some colleges and universities, and sometimes consortia of colleges and universities, sponsor on-campus visits by law school representatives as part of their graduate/professional school days. Whether you are just beginning college or you are an alumnus, you should check with universities in your area to see if they sponsor such local events.

For Applicants with Disabilities

Law school admission personnel and prelaw advisors are becoming increasingly knowledgeable about—and sensitive to—issues affecting students with disabilities. Moreover, if you have a disability, you may find it useful to talk to others who can offer guidance geared to your particular needs. There are two organizations that are helpful in this regard.

The American Council on Education operates the HEATH Resource Center, the national clearinghouse on postsecondary education for individuals with disabilities. HEATH can provide information about requesting disability-related accommodations, ascertaining the level of physical and programmatic access available at law schools, and thinking through disability issues surrounding the application process. A reprint of "Students with Disabilities and Law School" from the HEATH newsletter is available free by request. HEATH can be reached at One Dupont Circle NW, Suite 800, Washington DC 20036-1193. In the Washington, DC metropolitan area the center's phone number is 202.939.9320; outside Washington, the toll-free number is 800.54.HEATH. Both numbers are Voice/TDD.

The Association on Higher Education and Disability (AHEAD) is a nonprofit organization of persons from all 50 states, Canada, and other countries committed to promoting full participation of individuals with disabilities in college life. The association can be reached at P.O. Box 21192, Columbus, OH 43221-0192. You can also telephone the office at 614.488.4972 (Voice/TDD).

Council on Legal Education Opportunity (CLEO)

For over 20 years, CLEO has been helping students from economically and educationally disadvantaged backgrounds. Each year CLEO accepts a number of students to attend regional summer institutes around the United States. Students who successfully complete CLEO have an increased probability for admission to law schools around the country. For students who complete the CLEO program and enroll in law school, an allowance for living expenses is provided at the beginning of each semester of law school. Students who meet the CLEO guidelines should also consult *Thinking About Law School: A Minority Guide* for additional information about programs for minority students.

Other Sources of Information

Take advantage as well of library materials and any career resource centers or events in your community. Talk freely with any law school alumni that you know, but bear in mind that information about law schools can become outdated fairly quickly; talk to a recent graduate or one who is active in alumni affairs. Also keep in mind that your decision about which law school to choose should be based on your individual needs, not on someone else's opinion about what is best for you, or what was best for them. Always consider the source, and be sure to verify the accuracy of any word-of-mouth information conveyed to you.

Chapter 6

Evaluating Law Schools

Accreditation

The most important accrediting body in U.S. legal education is the American Bar Association (ABA). All ABA-approved law schools must meet minimum standards established by the ABA. These standards relate to faculty, curriculum, facilities, library holdings, and clinical programs. We strongly recommend that you first consider those schools that have been approved by the ABA. Other United States law schools may be accredited only by their state bar associations or not accredited all. There are serious professional risks in attending any school that does not have ABA approval. Please refer to Appendix A for more complete information on this subject.

The Federation of Law Societies in Canada has equivalent importance for that country's law schools. Canada has two legal traditions, the French civil-law tradition dominant in Quebec and the English common-law tradition dominant in the other provinces and territories. In order to practice law in Quebec, it is usually necessary to obtain a civil-law degree from a law school in Quebec or in the civil-law program of the University of Ottawa. To practice in common-law jurisdictions, it is usually necessary to obtain a degree from one of the common-law law schools referred to in the *LSAT Registration and Information Book—Canadian Edition.* More detailed information about requirements for practicing law can be obtained from the various provinces.

Ranking Law Schools: A Caveat

Be very careful of any book or magazine article that claims to be able to rank schools—for example, by referring to the "top 10" or "top 20" law schools in the country, or otherwise assigning a numerical ranking to a school (see page 46 in Chapter 5, "Other Publications," for additional discussion). Each student should use highly subjective criteria when determining which school is best for him or for her. The American Bar Association has this to say about law school rating systems:

No rating of law schools, beyond the simple statement
of their accreditation status, is attempted or advocated
by the official organizations in legal education. Qualities
that make one kind of school good for one student may
not be as important to another. ... Prospective law
students should consider a variety of factors in making
their choice among schools.

Robert Gibson, prelaw advisor at the State University of New
York at Albany, strongly counsels his students to alter their
thinking on the subject of ranking schools: "Perhaps the question
isn't where does the law school rank but how high will you rank
when you graduate from the school you choose?" he asks. He
further suggests that "how well you do is going to be heavily
influenced by your being comfortable [at the school you choose];
therefore, [such factors] as size, location, and so on" are of crucial
importance as a student evaluates a school.

Categories of Law Schools

There are many ways to take a school's measure. The best way to
evaluate which school is a match for you is to research accurate
details about specific schools that fit your needs and preferences
with regard to such things as location, class size, faculty/student
ratio, special programs, and other criteria discussed later in this
chapter. In the course of your research, however, you are bound to
come across references to such things as "big name" schools, or
schools that seem tied to a specialty area, such as international or
environmental law. We will briefly address some of these terms in
this section; however, the best advice about broad categorizations
of law schools is to **beware of labels**. As you will see, labels can
become very confusing, mainly because it is sometimes possible to
attach several labels to the same school. As with ranking schools,
your focus should remain on the specific criteria that makes a
school a good match for you, and not on any broad categorization
that may be ultimately misleading.

■ *Highly Competitive Schools*

Admittedly, there is a hierarchy of law schools based on GPAs and
LSAT scores of the first-year class, notable faculty, and the prestige

of the parent institution. We emphasize that it is difficult, if not impossible, to quantify strength of curriculum, teaching quality, job-placement services, libraries, nature of the student community and other such criteria discussed in this chapter; nevertheless, there are some obvious advantages to attending one of the highly competitive, prestigious schools—assuming you have the credentials to be admitted. For example, you can be assured that the quality of your education will be very high. A law degree from such a school might give you a competitive edge in your search for employment. In addition, starting salaries for graduates of these schools tend to be higher than the national average—mainly because the large, private law firms are more likely to recruit from these schools. Furthermore, many law students find that the high level of competition stimulates and challenges them to greater levels of achievement.

Why, then, would a qualified applicant choose **not** to attend a highly competitive school? First, the quality of education is not necessarily better than that of many other schools. Again, it is critically important that a student feel comfortable with the school's geographical, social, and intellectual environment. Some people find that the intense competition in the so-called top schools keeps them from doing their best work. Others are not interested in eventually practicing law at a large firm in a major city. In fact, some prefer to practice in their home states or regions.

In other words, the prestige or competitiveness of a law school should not be the sole—or even main—factor in deciding where to attend. Remember, your objective is to find the school or schools to match your needs.

■ *National, Regional, and Local Schools*

A **national** school will generally have an applicant population and a student body that draws almost indistinguishably from the nation as a whole and will have many international students as well. National schools also emphasize employment opportunities across the United States. A **regional** school is likely to have a population that is primarily from the geographic region of its location, though many regional schools have students from all over the country as well; a number of regional schools draw heavily from a particular geographical area, yet graduates may find jobs all over the country. Generally speaking, a **local** school is drawing primarily on applicants who either come from or want to practice in the proximate area in which the school is located. Many local law schools have excellent reputations and compete with the national schools in faculty salaries, in research-supporting activities, and in resources generally. Check the school's catalog or talk with the admission and placement staff to get a clear breakdown on where their students come from and where they are finding jobs.

■ *Specialty Schools*

Even if you're fairly certain of the kind of law you'd like to practice, it is unwise to consider specializing too much in law school. As we discussed in Chapter 2, many lawyers don't begin to choose a specialty until they've been practicing for at least several years. Keep in mind that a well-rounded legal education gives you the flexibility to consider many career options. Of course, it's reasonable to take note of schools offering many electives in a field that interests you (see page 62, "Availability of Courses") By checking the catalog, you also can learn how many faculty members are identified with that field. "If a student feels strongly that there is some area that he or she is interested in, it's worth finding out whether there are schools that are strong in those areas," says Susan Krinsky, associate dean of admissions at Tulane University. "But," she cautions, "often the specialties really depend on the faculty member who happens to be there, and it would be really hard for a prospective student to find out whether environmental law, for example, [is stressed] at [a particular] school because of the particular faculty member or whether it's there because of a commitment on the part of the administration, and whether if [that] faculty member should leave, [the law school] will [recruit] some other faculty member to continue that specialty, or whether that specialty is just going to disappear."

Krinsky adds one more word of advice: Find out "whether the school has other strengths as well, in case it turns out you're not interested in [that specialty]. You never know, you might find yourself extraordinarily interested in [another subject entirely]."

In general, however, most prelaw advisors counsel students not to apply to a particular school in order to become a specialist in any area of law.

■ *Part-time and Evening Programs*

Part-time programs may be offered either in the evening or day, and part-time law students generally receive the same quality of education as their full-time counterparts. Approximately 16 percent of law students currently enroll in part-time programs; the course of study usually takes four years to complete instead of three. As a general rule, part-time students seem to have the same success in finding jobs as those students enrolled in full-time study.

The conventional wisdom is that if it's possible to attend law school on a full-time basis, you should do so. Full-time study allows total immersion in the study of law as well as full participation in the various organizations and associations on campus. You are likely to benefit from a greater selection of clinical education courses to sharpen your lawyering skills. Furthermore, only about 40 percent of the law schools offer part-time programs, so your options are automatically limited.

Nevertheless, thousands of students graduate from part-time programs each year, and educators often cite the exceptional commitment, dedication, and tenacity of these students. Often part-time students, working at other jobs, possess valuable insights into the practical application of legal concepts and practices.

Some students enter law school on a full-time basis only to find that personal circumstances force them to transfer to a part-time program. If you suspect this could happen to you, it is advisable to consider a law school that offers a part-time program. Also be aware that it is unlikely that your job will be able to cover normal living expenses combined with law school expenses. You may still require some form of financial assistance (see Chapter 8).

Criteria for Evaluating Specific Law Schools

This section offers practical guidelines for assessing the facilities, student body, faculty, and other resources of law schools. Use all of the research sources we describe in this chapter to assist you. For additional information about the topics in this section, consult *The Official Guide to U.S. Law Schools,* published by Law Services.

■ *Location*

Donald Racheter, director of the prelaw program at the Central University of Iowa, has observed a lack of awareness on the part of many students on the question of law school locale. He remarks: "The [students] either want to go to the [so-called] top ten [law schools] or they want to go to the local [schools]. They don't really have a good conception that there are 176 ABA-approved schools to choose from. ... They either settle for what's close by and familiar or they've got these unrealistic expectations. They've got to understand that there is a whole range of schools out there, and they've got to have a better search strategy." Numerous prelaw advisors concurred on this point, with one going so far as to state wryly, "I give geography lessons to my students as part of my orientation to law schools," (see Appendixes F and G).

There are those students, nonetheless, who may well regard the decision to attend law school as—among other things—an opportunity for change and who want to seriously explore schools located in another part of the country. These students may want to give some thought to such things as preferred climate, preference of urban or rural environment, and preference of a large or small city—what a number of prelaw advisors emphasize as "the personal factors." Many applicants consider the location of a law school to be the most important ingredient in the evaluation process. Let us discuss briefly some of the factors that can influence your decision about where to attend law school.

Employment and marital status. If you or your spouse (or partner) has a full-time job you cannot or do not wish to leave, your choice of law schools is obviously limited to the region in which you currently reside. Conversely, students who plan to relocate with a family may need to explore job opportunities for a working spouse, and school opportunities for children.

One word of caution: do not attempt to attend law school full time while working at a full-time job. In fact, ABA approval precludes schools from allowing full-time students to work for more than 20 hours per week, and students are discouraged from working at all their first year.

Ethnic, racial, and cultural background. The social atmosphere of a school (and its surrounding environment) may be something you will want to consider. You can find out specific information about minority enrollment by consulting *The Official Guide to U.S. Law*

Schools, or by contacting the school directly. See also *Thinking About Law School: A Minority Guide,* published by Law Services.

Region in which you plan to practice. You may know—or think you know—the type of law you would like to practice and the place you would like to practice it. In fact, you may have already established a client base and potential business contacts in your hometown or some other region. Remember, however, that you will spend at least three years in law school (more if you go part time), and much can change within that time. Think carefully before making a commitment that will significantly affect the rest of your life. One more point: it is **not** necessary to go to law school in the state in which you plan to practice. In fact, some states do not have a law school within their boundaries. As we discuss in Chapter 10, ABA-approved schools do not emphasize the laws of the state in the overall curriculum. There may be some coursework available, but it is not until you take the bar examination in a particular state that you fully prepare yourself for learning this particularized material. (See Chapter 10 for more on preparing for the bar exam.)

On the other hand, you may want to apply to a school in a region with a growing economy as part of your overall career-planning strategy. This can be especially useful if you are undecided about where to apply; if you can relocate easily; and if your credentials are not as strong as they could be. You will need to do careful research, however, and understand that economic growth can be cyclical, sporadic, and sometimes unpredictable. A site visit can be especially useful in this case.

Applicants with disabilities. If you rely on a wheelchair or crutches, the accessibility of facilities and programs and the topography of the campus can be an important factor in choosing a law school. If you need other types of accommodations—such as readers, interpreters, or courseload modifications—it will be important to know the level of support available. (See Chapter 5 for more information on resources for students with disabilities.)

Cost. The cost of tuition can vary from school to school. Also, some parts of the country are more costly to live in than others. The cost at a state-supported school is likely to be lower for state residents than for those out of state. See Chapter 8 for a more complete discussion of the financial aspect of attending law school.

Housing. You will want to explore the availability of reasonably priced housing and transportation. Is on-campus housing available? Is there affordable, safe housing close to the campus? If you have to live farther off campus, is there adequate public transportation? Will you need a car?

■ *School Size*

The size of a law school can be an important factor in your evaluation process. Chances are, the larger the enrollment, the more diverse the student body. Not surprisingly, larger law schools also tend to offer a greater selection of courses. But it is the size of the section (the traveling homeroom of students who take most of the first-year courses together) which determines much of the intimacy and quality of first-year life. Much of the learning in law school depends on the quality of class discussion—which is frequently affected by the size of the class. The catalog of one prominent law school maintains that a class with more than 40 students is probably too large for a roundtable discussion. On the other hand, one noted legal educator contends that he can't teach his class in contracts with *only* 40 students: he feels he needs more to produce a good mix of reactions, opinions, and criticism. Of course, size is a personal as well as an academic consideration. A shy graduate of a small college might be overwhelmed at a larger law school—in which some students would thrive. However, even the largest law school is much smaller than most small colleges.

The parent university. About 90 percent of ABA-approved law schools are part of a larger university. A parent university can offer certain advantages to law students—especially if it is located on the same grounds as the law school. For example, a parent university presents more opportunities for academic and social events, campus theater groups, sports teams, and other activities associated with student life. Certainly it offers the opportunity to meet people other than those pursuing a law career. In addition, a law school affiliated with a university may offer more options for joint-degree programs (see pages 64-65) and for taking nonlaw courses that are credited toward the J.D. degree. Also, if the parent university's undergraduate college is considered outstanding, the law school may benefit from its reputation.

■ *Student Body*

Law schools generally strive to attain a balanced student body that reflects a variety of backgrounds and experiences. This can be advantageous to all students: the broader the spectrum of student interests and training, the richer the educational opportunities. In any case, think of selecting a law school in which you are intellectually challenged and stimulated by your classmates.

In addition to gathering information from catalogs and site visits, you will find it valuable to talk to prelaw advisors, alumni, law school admission offices, and—most important—the students themselves. All of these resources will help you develop a profile of a school's student body.

■ *Faculty*

It is difficult to assess individual faculty members before you enter the school. School catalogs will give you some idea of the backgrounds of the full-time faculty—such as their alma maters, fields of specialty, and unique accomplishments. You may also want to speak with students who are currently enrolled in the school, if possible. For additional information about individual teachers, check the latest edition of the Association of American Law School's *Directory of Law Teachers* published by West Publishing Company. This book is available at local libraries and may also be purchased.

Here are the kinds of questions you can ask to develop a profile of a law school's faculty:

Educational background. Where were the faculty members educated? Do they represent a diversity of schools? Do some members of the faculty have additional graduate training? Also, consider the diversity of professional degrees among the faculty. For example, are there some faculty members with a master's degree in law (LL.M.)? Are there a few interdisciplinary degrees such as the M.A., M.D., or Ph.D.?

Professional experience. Remember that law schools are professional schools. Experienced faculties often have been exposed to a wide range of legal activities, and that exposure can enrich your legal education significantly. Keep the following questions in mind: Have faculty members worked in private practice, for state or federal agencies, and for corporations? How many have served on the bench and in other judicial capacities? How many have dealt with disadvantaged and minority groups or headed commissions and study groups?

Professional reputation. Are the teachers recognized as authorities in their fields by virtue of their writings and professional activities? Have they written casebooks, studies, treatises, and articles that are widely respected and used? At what other schools have the professors taught? Are they invited to serve as guest lecturers, to deliver major addresses, or to serve as visiting professors at other law schools? Have they been involved in law reform?

Heterogeneity of faculty mix. The ethnic and racial background—or the gender balance—of the faculty may be especially important to you. A faculty with a diverse profile can further serve to enrich your legal education by exposing you to educators with different perspectives, approaches, and values. (Again, consult *Thinking About Law School: A Minority Guide* for further discussion of this subject.)

Faculty/student relationships. Do the faculty "stars" actually teach the basic courses, or do they work primarily on their own research and writing? You may find that the faculty members with outstanding credentials may be inaccessible; they may even be ineffective teachers. Unfortunately, you probably won't be able to learn this information from a law school catalog. It's best to visit the campus and talk to the students directly. Other campus-based sources of information include the student newspaper, the student bar association, and (perhaps best of all) student reviews of faculty members, which may be on deposit in the law library.

Faculty/student ratio. Try to ascertain the ratio between full-time professors and students. Full-time rather than adjunct faculty comprise the core of any law school teaching staff. A school with a large student body and only a few professors presents a slim hope for individual-student attention and small seminars. The majority of ABA-approved law schools do not exceed a ratio of 30 students to one faculty member. Although some of the most competitive law schools have large sections in the introductory courses, keep in mind that they also offer smaller classes, clinics, simulations, and seminars in advanced-level subjects. Look for opportunities for small-group courses and individual supervision. Another advantage of large faculties is that they allow for faculty specialization in a broad range of subject matters and for varieties of teaching technique; in addition, they encourage cross-fertilization of ideas among faculty members in all fields. A free and full exchange is critical to the flourishing of any law school.

- **The Library**

Since you can expect to spend a great deal of time in the library, it pays to evaluate this facility carefully. Below are a few important considerations:

Library holdings. All ABA-approved law schools must maintain a library that houses research materials deemed essential for the study of law. These materials include digests of federal and state cases; decisions by the Supreme Court, federal and state courts, and other courts; codes of federal and state rules and statutes; reports on English case law; and a variety of legal publications and journals. Beyond these resources, a good law school library will maintain special collections that adequately support the specialized programs offered by the law school. Many law school libraries are Congressional depositories. Also, law school libraries generally subscribe to a computerized legal research service, such as LEXIS or WESTLAW.

Availability of books. A good law school library not only maintains an adequate range of reference works, it also houses sufficient copies of each book—particularly the most popular reference materials. Multiple sets of frequently used books are essential.

Catalog system and librarian expertise. Even if the library has all the resources you need, you won't be able to gain access to them readily if the catalog system is disorganized or out of date. Also, try to learn how many professional research librarians are available to help you. Don't forget that the staff must be large enough to meet the special needs of students and faculty alike.

Research resources in the surrounding community. If you attend law school in Washington, DC, for example, you'll have a wealth of resources at your fingertips—not to mention a chance to audit Supreme Court arguments and Congressional debates. New York offers the United Nations among other resources. Students should consider the legislative resources of state capitals as well as the trial and appellate court system in most urban centers. Most large cities have valuable legal holdings in the public libraries. Other libraries on campus may also be extremely helpful, and law schools cooperate with interlibrary loans.

Comfort and accessibility. Because you are likely to spend considerable time in the library, the facility should have an adequate number of comfortable seats that can withstand the test of time, and it should be well lit. Also, according to ABA standards, a law school library should be able to accommodate at least 50 percent of the total enrollment of full-time students, and 35 percent of the total enrollment of students in the evening programs, if applicable. Furthermore, the library should remain open long enough each day to accommodate just about any student's schedule. It should open its doors by the start of classes and remain open well into the night.

- *Availability of Courses*

Some questions to ask regarding course selection are these: Does the school offer a wide variety of courses, or does it offer only a narrow range of required courses, a few electives, and an even more restricted seminar program? Do courses offer adequate opportunity for writing experiences? Does the curriculum include individual courses on rapidly emerging fields, such as environmental law, transnational law, health law, immigration law, urban housing and redevelopment, juvenile rights, white collar criminal prosecution and defense, computer/technology law, and corporate reorganization? Are seminars held in important and expanding areas of the law? Does the school seem likely to keep pace with new trends in legal education? Are all courses listed in the catalog taught on a regular basis?

- *Career Services*

What kind of career service does the school offer? Find out the range of employers who come to interview at the school, and the extent and quality of career counseling offered there. Ask about the school's alumni ties. Find out the range of services offered: Schools may arrange panel presentations or meetings with lawyers who practice in different fields; they may offer workshops on job-search strategies. Most law schools keep some statistics on what happens to its students following graduation, including what percentage it placed, what kinds of jobs they have taken and where, and what kinds of salaries they are making. Find out what happens to the school's best graduates, and what happens to its average or below-average students. But remember that statistics can be misleading. Many of the career services statistics are compiled from questionnaires sent to graduates in the years following their departure from law school. In order to value those statistics correctly, you would need to know what percentage of all students responded to the questionnaires. Also, how vigorously did the placement staff follow up on the students? Some students who have failed to secure a job offer by graduation may be offered a job six months later, following their successful passage of the bar exam.

■ *Additional Areas for Exploration*

Clinical-education programs. Years ago law students were educated only in classrooms, and much of what they learned was rather abstract and theoretical. Since the 1970s, however, the introduction of clinical-education programs at most law schools has placed a greater emphasis on the practical application of lawyering skills—both in and out of the classroom.

According to Susan Westerberg Prager, a former president of the Association of American Law Schools, the organizing principle of clinical education is "the introduction of 'the client' into our schools. Students quickly learn that they desperately need more than the ability to identify issues and engage in doctrinal analysis if they are to be responsive to a client."

Essentially, there can be three types of clinics within a clinical education program: internal, external, and simulated clinics. **Internal clinics** are usually conducted at the law school and are supervised by a faculty member. Clients come to the student clinic for legal services, sometimes limited to a specific field of law. **External or placement clinics**, sometimes called **externships**, are those that take place away from the law school. The supervising faculty member usually is present on site. A **simulated clinic** may make use of role playing and electronic equipment, such as video recorders and laser disks, to help refine skills in interviewing, negotiating, trial advocacy, and arbitration.

Both internal and external clinics give students the opportunity to work on actual cases with actual clients—under the supervision of the law school's faculty. These clinics also introduce students to a wide range of clients in need of different kinds of expertise: you might work in the office of the district attorney or public defender; you might work for a profit or nonprofit organization; your casework might focus on environmental law, community law, family law, or corporate law.

Here are a few questions to ask when evaluating a school's clinical program:

- How does the school define a clinic? There is wide-ranging debate on what makes a good clinic. Some law school deans feel that a good clinical-education program will feature internal and external clinics with actual cases and actual clients; others point to outstanding programs that rely heavily on simulation. Try to find out as much as you can about the strengths of a school's particular clinical program.
- How many clinics tend to be offered each year, and how diverse are they? The answer to these questions may tell you something about the law school's commitment to its clinical-education program and how the school utilizes resources in the community.
- Is there a classroom component before, during, and/or after the clinic? Classroom discussion of the clinical experience—including seminars and symposia—will maximize the educational value of the clinic and enhance your ability to draw general conclusions from your experience.
- What is the relationship of the full-time faculty to the clinic? Some law schools rotate full-time faculty in and out of the clinical-education programs to keep the programs fresh, diverse, and adequately staffed.
- What is the student-faculty ratio in the clinics? The smaller the ratio, the better. A faculty-student ratio of 1:8 is the norm, and few, if any, programs improve upon that ratio.
- Do the clinics offer credits toward graduation?

Again, you can find the answers to these questions and others either in the law school catalog, the school descriptions section of *The Official Guide to U.S. Law Schools,* or the law school admission offices.

Combined-degree programs. Dual-degree programs allow you to acquire a J.D. and an advanced degree in another field in less time than it would take to acquire the two separately. For example, a typical J.D./M.B.A program—one of the most common of this type—condenses the three-year law program and the two-year business administration program into a single four-year course of study. Such interdisciplinary legal education may become increasingly important as the nature of the lawyer's tasks coincides with that of the economist, policy maker, political scientist, and businessperson. The degree earned might be a J.D./M.A. or J.D./Ph.D., as well as J.D./M.D., a J.D./M.P.A. (Masters in Public Administration), or a J.D./M.S. (in social work or public policy, for example).

If you choose to apply to a dual-degree program, seek out some career guidance before you decide. If you are interested in a dual-degree program, inquire at the schools about admission requirements. Pay particular attention to the issue of timing: Some law schools require that joint-degree candidates begin their studies at the law school.

Find out from the schools what kinds of jobs their dual-degree students are getting when they graduate. Talk also with both graduates of the program and current students: Are they satisfied with the program?

Be sure to check the reputation of the school offering the other degree as well as the law school. Different schools within the same university may have widely different reputations. This will affect the value of the combined program.

You should also talk with lawyers who practice in the field that interests you and ask whether the dual-degree program is likely to increase your chances of getting a job in that field. There are no jobs that specifically **require** a dual degree, points out Joseph Burns, prelaw advisor at Boston College. Who, then, are the people who go for those degrees? "People who are headed for high-level corporate positions, for whom [that] credential is a plus...," suggests Burns. "People who. ... [want to be) leaders or policy makers..." Others say it may have to do with (perceived or real) gaps in a student's undergraduate education. Some simply elect to combine degrees for their own educational benefit.

There is a fair amount of dispute on the subject of the usefulness or practicality of the dual degree. It may, for example, be possible to take several courses in the other department, counted toward the J.D. degree, but without investing an additional year to get the other degree. In the final analysis, the decision depends on your specific interests and needs. Again, the more you will be able to clarify those interests and needs, the better you are able to determine the value of pursuing a particular path.

Academic assistance programs. Programs for students who need or who are expected to need assistance with legal analysis and writing are offered by most law schools. Students are invited to participate in these programs on the basis of either their entering credentials or their demonstrated academic performance. This assistance may be offered in the summer prior to beginning law school, during the academic year, or both. The aim of academic assistance programs is to ensure that students have an equal opportunity to compete in law school. For further information about academic assistance programs, consult the admission office at the law school.

Visiting faculty. Are adjunct professors assigned primarily to basic courses rather than to specialized electives? If so, this might be due to the school's shortage of full-time faculty—or it may be because too many full-time faculty are on leave.

Student law journals. How many are published and what are their strengths? The journals often reflect curriculum emphasis, student interests, and intellectual diversity.

Student organizations. You can also tell something about a law school's intellectual resources—and its students—by the number and range of student associations and organizations sponsored on campus. Many schools have chapters of the American Bar Association/Law Student Division, a student bar association, associations for minority-group students, a Women's Law Association, a gay and lesbian law student society, and associations based on religious affiliations and professional fraternities. There are other types of organizations to be found on a law school campus; for example, a legal-assistance society for low-income people, a postconviction-assistance project, a volunteer income tax assistance program, a law student spouses' club, an international-law society, a law and technology society, a client-counseling society, a trial-advocacy society, an entertainment and sports law society, and various political groups.

In this chapter, you have read about **information**—what kind of information is useful to you in selecting a law school and where to go for that information. Perhaps you are beginning to form an idea of the kind of school you hope to attend; you may even have assembled a good-sized list of schools that could fit the bill. If so—or in anticipation of doing so—you are ready to move to the next step: narrowing the field to a few well-chosen law schools that meet your needs, and preparing your application material. The following chapter discusses strategies and tips for making your final selection, and takes you through the specific steps of readying your application.

Chapter 7

Selecting and Applying to Law Schools

Using Admission Profile Grids to Assess Your Chances of Admission

The admission process is more than a numbers game, as we've pointed out in Chapter 4; however, your LSAT score and your GPA are used in combination by most law schools as a starting place for their careful evaluation of your qualifications. These two numerical scores reflect **whether you are in the range of competition** at a school.

In the course of researching the schools that interest you, you should certainly try to learn if your numbers put you in the acceptable range of that school's admission qualifications. *The Official Guide to U.S. Law Schools* can be quite helpful in this regard. As you read the profiles of the various schools listed in the *Official Guide*, you will see that most schools provide a grid that tells you how many persons applied and how many were admitted in a range of LSAT scores and GPAs.

Using these grids along with all the other information you have gathered about each school, you should be able roughly to determine your chances of being admitted to a school.

Applying to a Cross-section of Schools

To how many schools should you apply? There is no one right answer as there are a number of factors to be considered. If you are unable to relocate, your choices are obviously limited. Each school requires an application fee. Applying to several schools adds up to a few hundred dollars very quickly; therefore, you are not likely to apply to every school that interests you. Then, too, you may be uncertain about where you would like to attend. Adequate research will help you to develop more than one obvious choice.

Most applicants narrow their selections to four to six schools. Partly this is because various schools may have appeal for different reasons. But the best reason to submit more than one application is to increase your chance of admission. Applying to 10 schools that are beyond your reach is not the best method to assure a good result. The best strategy is to apply to at least one school you consider a long-shot (but not impossible), several where you seem to have about an even chance of admission, and at least one where admission seems probable. In other words, dream a little, be realistic, and be safe.

Dream a little. It's certainly reasonable to apply to one or two schools you greatly admire—even if your chances for admission are not especially solid. "Dream" schools are those where the applicant has a 20 to 50 percent chance of acceptance. Certainly, if you've done a good job of supplementing your academic credentials with a clear and compelling personal essay and strong letters of recommendation, you are more likely to realize your dream.

Be realistic. Of course, it's wise to send the majority of applications to schools where your chances of admission are good. Again, if you have a sound self-assessment (see Chapter 4) and you do your research effectively, you will know which schools these are. They are generally schools where you have a 50 to 80 percent chance of acceptance.

Be safe. It is extremely important that you apply to at least one backup school. Generally speaking, these are schools where you have an 80 to 100 percent chance of acceptance, based on admission profiles of the LSAT scores and GPAs of admitted students. Applying to a backup or "safety" school is more than just a security measure. Just one acceptance letter can greatly ease the tension as you are anxiously awaiting news from your first and second choices. You must choose your backup school as carefully as your other selections. An acceptance letter is meaningless if you do not want to attend the school.

The Application Process

The law school application must be obtained by you directly from the admission office of each school to which you apply. It will be up to you to mail that application back to the admission office when you have completed it. Application fees vary from school to school. Many schools waive their application fees for applicants who would otherwise be unable to apply. Be sure to follow an individual school's application instructions.

Much of your correspondence will be directed to Law Services in Newtown, Pennsylvania, which provides admission-related services to law schools and applicants. Below is a description of the forms you must complete as you begin applying to law schools, as well as the documents that Law Services will compile on your behalf. Tables 7.1 and 7.2 on the following pages will help you organize a schedule to meet the appropriate deadlines.

■ *Forms to Be Completed by the Applicant*

The following forms and detailed information about completing them can be found in the *LSAT/LSDAS Registration and Information Book*, which is updated annually and may be obtained from undergraduate prelaw advising offices, law schools, or Law Services. The *Registration and Information Book* also discusses any fees that apply. **Be sure to type or clearly print all information unless you are otherwise instructed.** Law Services' policies and fees are subject to change, so be sure to obtain the current *Registration and Information Book* for the period in which you are applying to law school.

LSAT/LSDAS Registration Form. Use this form to register for the LSAT and to subscribe to the Law School Data Assembly Service (LSDAS). (See below for more information.) You need not do both at the same time. Use law school application deadlines to determine when you should begin your 12-month subscription to LSDAS.

Transcript request forms. Send these forms to all undergraduate, graduate, and professional schools where you have completed coursework and received academic credit. You should have completed at least six semesters of undergraduate work before requesting that transcripts be sent to Law Services. **Do not send your own transcripts to Law Services; they will be returned unprocessed.**

Academic Record Form. Complete this form if (a) you have attended more institutions than can be listed in the LSDAS section of the LSAT/LSDAS Registration Form, or (b) you are unable to obtain a transcript from an institution you have attended due to an outstanding financial obligation. Submit the academic record form with your completed registration form.

Application Matching Forms. You must include an application matching form with every application you send to a law school.

Table 7.1
Using October or December 1993 Test for Fall 1994 Admission

August/September		October/November	December	January
Prepare for the LSAT →	Receive an LSDAS Subscription Confirmation letter →	Take the LSAT →	Send application to law school(s)—include application matching form	Receive December LSAT score →
Research law schools — select those to which you will apply →	Receive a Law Services Activity Update that indicates activity that has occurred in your file →	Receive your LSAT score →	Take the December LSAT, if applicable →	Receive a Law Services Activity Update that indicates LSDAS Law School Report has been sent to law school(s)
Compose a schedule of application deadlines →		Register for December LSAT, if applicable →		
Register for the LSAT and subscribe to LSDAS →	Send transcript request forms to undergraduate, graduate, and law school/professional schools. (Once Law Services receives official transcripts, it takes approximately two weeks to process them.)	Receive a Law Services Activity Update that indicates receipt of official transcripts →		
Receive an LSAT Admission Ticket		Receive a Master Law School Report once all undergraduate transcripts have been summarized		

Application deadlines vary, but most law schools suggest applying as early as possible.
This example presents one of many approaches to the law school admission process; it is important for you to prepare your own timetable based on the application deadlines for the law schools to which you apply.

Table 7.2
Using June 1993 Test for Fall 1994 Admission

April/May	June	Late July/August	September	October/November	November/December
Prepare for the LSAT	Take the LSAT	Receive your LSAT score	Subscribe to LSDAS	Take the October LSAT, if repeating the test	Receive October LSAT score
Register for the LSAT	Receive a Law Services Activity Update	Research law schools—select those to which you will apply	Receive an LSDAS Subscription Confirmation letter	Send application to law school(s)—include application matching form	Receive a Law Services Activity Update that indicates LSDAS Law School Report has been sent to law school(s)
Receive an LSAT Admission Ticket		Compose a schedule of application deadlines	Send transcript request forms to undergraduate, graduate, and law school/professional schools. (Once Law Services receives official transcripts, it takes approximately two weeks to process them.)	Receive a Law Services Activity Update that indicates Law Services' receipt of transcripts	
		Register for October LSAT, if repeating the test	Receive a Law Services Activity Update that indicates activity that has occurred in your file	Receive a Master Law School Report once all undergraduate transcripts have been summarized	
		Receive a Law Services Activity Update			

Application deadlines vary, but most law schools suggest applying as early as possible.
This example presents one of many approaches to the law school admission process; it is important for you to prepare your own timetable based on the application deadlines for the law schools to which you apply.

■ *Reports to Be Completed by Law Services*

The Law School Data Assembly Service (LSDAS) provides a means of centralizing and standardizing undergraduate academic records to simplify the law school admission process. The LSDAS prepares and provides an LSDAS Law School Report for each law school to which a subscriber applies. The LSDAS Law School Report contains:

- biographic information
- a year-by-year, college-by-college summary of your undergraduate grades
- photocopies of each transcript sent to Law Services
- your current test score; reportable test results for the last five years, up to 12 (including cancellations and absences), and an average LSAT score, if applicable
- photocopies of your most recent LSAT writing samples, with a limit of three
- an admission index (see below for explanation), if requested by the law school
- special documents, such as a letter from a certified professional regarding a disability or a letter from Law Services regarding conditions during a particular test administration (sent only at applicant's request)

■ *Fee Waivers*

In cases of extreme economic hardship, Law School Admission Services will waive fees for LSAT registration and LSDAS subscription. You may request a fee waiver for these services through any member law school's admission office, even one to which you do not ultimately apply. The *LSAT/LSDAS Registration and Information Book* contains current information regarding fee waivers. Be sure to submit your request well in advance of the LSAT registration deadline listed in the *LSAT/LSDAS Registration and Information Book*.

■ *Admission Index*

Some law schools combine the LSAT score(s) and GPA to produce a single number called an index to assist in comparing applicants. If a school decides to use an index formula, Law Services calculates and reports each candidate's index to the school as part of the LSDAS Law School Report. For more information on the index, consult the *LSAT/LSDAS Registration and Information Book.*

■ *Candidate Referral Service (CRS)*

The Candidate Referral Service (CRS) gives you the option of letting the law schools choose you; this is especially useful if you are not sure where you want to apply. It works like this: A law school can search the data file for applicants whose credentials meet its particular standards and student profile. Depending on the school, applicants may be recruited on the basis of racial, ethnic, economic, and geographic background as well as GPA and LSAT score. To participate in the CRS, simply check the appropriate space on your LSAT/LSDAS Order Form. Law schools then may contact you with an invitation to apply. Such an invitation indicates that the school considers you a **likely** candidate for admission; however, an invitation does not **guarantee** admission. If the school appeals to you, it is wise to submit an application form as soon as possible. Don't worry if you do not receive inquiries from schools that interest you. Some schools do not use CRS extensively.

The Law School Application

Each school only knows as much about you as can be surmised from your application file. The LSDAS Report presents only the sketchiest numerical and demographic information; your report could be similar to that of many other people. If schools are going to have any detail about who you are, they will have to learn it from you.

Your personal statement and letters of recommendation offer you the opportunity to craft your application with a shape and a direction. Think of this task as a combination of planning and advocacy, the two skills most central to a lawyer's work. You are the one who gets to make the case; don't waste the opportunity.

■ *The Personal Statement*

Your personal statement is one part of your law school application that allows you to describe yourself to admission officers in your own terms. This is an opportunity to **elaborate** on specific areas and address particular issues that the application form may not give you the opportunity to address. For example, if you've been able to overcome extenuating circumstances—such as extraordinary family responsibility, or a disability—you may **choose** to write about it as a measure of your strength of character, determination, and perseverance.[1] You may also want to bring together facts that appear in very different places in your file to form a coherent picture of you, the applicant. This is your chance to exercise some control, to lead the reader through your application, highlighting those areas that you feel deserve more emphasis. However, warns Sybil Richards, director of admissions at the University of Tennessee, "personal statements that simply reiterate whatever is on the application don't do anything for the applicant." The personal statement should be able to stand on its own as a compelling document. In a good personal statement, says Richards, "what stands out is the writing ... not so much what they say, but how well they say it."

The personal statement is especially important when you consider that most law schools do not include formal interviews as part of the admission process. Therefore, think of the personal statement as an interview—a chance to tell admission personnel who you are and what you have done that makes you uniquely qualified to study and practice law.

If there are weak areas in your application—and there are bound to be some—this is your opportunity to introduce that weakness on your terms, and defuse it. It is part of the job of the admission file reader to look for weak areas; you may as well frame the discussion yourself and offer reasonable and informative explanations. However, you don't want to spend an entire page trying to justify poor grades or a low LSAT score. Additionally, this is your opportunity to demonstrate your persuasiveness in discussing your own candidacy; some have called the personal statement the applicant's first case.

Keep two guidelines in mind: *write about yourself* and *be specific.* Admission personnel do not want to read your theories about theology and the universe or law and society. They want to read

---

[1]The recently enacted Americans with Disabilities Act, along with the Rehabilitation Act of 1973, provides protection against discrimination on the basis of disabilities. This protection extends to the admission decision-making process and provision of educational services. Students with disabilities may, however, request accommodation of their disability from the schools to which they have been admitted and that they wish to attend prior to the provision of any such accommodations.

about you. Be specific and concrete. State, and evaluate. You are a story teller; you want a specific character, a living person—you—to emerge from your telling. Don't just say you were in a particular club or association without explaining the purpose of the club or your role in it.

Style and tone. Your personal statement is not merely a writing sample. If it were, you would be permitted to submit a term paper, short story, newspaper article, or other such examples of your writing. However, it is *also* a writing sample—in addition to being a vehicle for stating your case. That means it should reflect your ability to write clearly and concisely; it should be grammatically correct and free of spelling errors. It must be your own work, but you can certainly discuss it with others; you may want to ask for feedback from someone whose judgment you trust. Unlike the writing sample on the LSAT, you have the luxury of time in this instance; you can revise, work on drafts of your statement, and proofread it carefully for errors before sending it out. You should maintain a positive, confident tone, but do not confuse confidence with arrogance.

Format. Follow any directions given by the particular law school on the application form. Generally, you should type the statement, with double spacing, and keep it to approximately two pages in length. Admission personnel may read thousands of these statements as they review applications each year. Aim to be clear, concise, and compelling. A memorable essay alone cannot compensate for an otherwise forgettable law school application—but it just might tip the scales in your favor if your application is hanging in the balance.

■ *Letters of Recommendation*

Letters of recommendation provide admission personnel with yet another perspective of your work and special qualities—usually through the written assessment of a college professor and/or employer. Because such letters are almost always positive, admission officers look for specific examples that clearly highlight your leadership capabilities, creativity, judgment, outstanding motivation, unusual intellectual curiosity, and excellent communication skills.

Some schools will enclose an evaluation checklist with the application form, asking the letter writer to assess the applicant in terms of specific personal qualities, such as:

- Esteem in which you are held by your peers
- Esteem in which you are held by faculty and other supervisors
- Ability to communicate orally and in writing
- Emotional stability and maturity
- Ability to work with others
- Leadership potential
- Creativity (including ability to see implications and synthesize ideas)
- Industry, initiative, motivation
- Judgment
- Honesty, integrity, trustworthiness

The letter writer may be asked to rate the applicant on a scale, or to choose from a list of words such as "extraordinary," "above average," "average," "no basis for judgment," and so on. Naturally, you will want to select someone who can recommend you highly, without qualification, and with enthusiasm. If a form letter such as the one described is used, select someone who you can be sure will consistently place you in the top categories.

Who should write letters of recommendation. Since law schools are academic institutions interested in your academic potential, university and college faculty will tend to carry the most weight with law school personnel. You should, therefore, have at least one letter from a professor in your major field of study; even if you've been out of school for a while, it's worth the effort to try and secure a letter from a teacher, if at all possible.

This person should know you fairly well, particularly your academic potential. The best letter writers are those who have written letters of recommendation previously for other former students, and who are willing to compare you favorably with those former students. The more specific the letter, with information on academic and personal interaction, the better.

Letters from employers can also be valuable if they cite specific examples of your outstanding character traits and personal accomplishments—including your ability to write, analyze, and make difficult decisions about complex matters.

Sybil Richards comments on what kind of letters she looks for: "The letter ... from a friend of a friend of a friend, who happens to be an attorney, doesn't tell us anything and shouldn't be given any weight at all." She looks, instead, for letters that are "completely detailed and provide an explanation of the applicant on a very objective basis." Dean Krinsky points out, as well, that it may not be the entire letter than makes an impact, but "often it's one sentence in a letter of recommendation that really alerts me that this is somebody special, somebody I'd want to be at my school." Likewise, letters from relatives, friends, and politicians for whom you have not worked have almost no value. If you are unable to provide a letter of recommendation from a faculty member or an employer, you may want to offer an explanation to the law school to which you are applying. A law school that requires letters of recommendation may insist that you do so.

Contacting letter writers. You may assist your letter writers by providing them with a résumé or discussing with them your own goals for the future. You may want to give them a copy of your personal statement as well. However, it is not advisable to ghost-write your own letters of recommendation, even if your reference sources agree to sign their names. Also, be certain that any personal relationship between you and your letter writer is disclosed.

Submitting letters of recommendation. As we discuss below, there are advantages to submitting your completed law school application as early as possible. In order to expedite the transmission of your letters of recommendation to prospective law schools, consider waiving your right to screen the letters. You can do so by signing a form supplied by the law school to which you are applying. Take advantage of the credential file services at the career or placement office of your undergraduate school. The office may forward your complete file of recommendations to each law school you specify.

Which law schools want letters? A number of law schools admit they do not consider letters of recommendation in the admission process. Others ask for letters but use them only to distinguish among applicants with similar test scores and grade rankings. However, many law schools—including some of the most highly competitive—regard letters of recommendation as a vital component of the admission process. In any case, you are wise to obtain the best letters of recommendation you can.

Additional Tips: Steering Clear of Common Pitfalls

■ *Read Directions Carefully to Avoid Clerical Delays*

You can facilitate the process of registering for the LSAT and subscribing to the LSDAS by taking the time to read and understand all the material in your *LSAT/LSDAS Registration and Information Book*. Many applicants fill out their subscription forms incorrectly because they haven't followed all the directions. As a result, they needlessly delay the processing of their applications. Some LSAT results are delayed because the answer sheets are filled out improperly. You may also delay the review of your file if you fail to have all of your undergraduate, graduate, and professional transcripts sent to Law Services. For example, you must send Transcript Request Forms to schools from which you have transferred or to schools where you were enrolled in summer sessions. Otherwise, it's possible that your LSDAS report will be sent to a prospective law school with the designation *unacknowledged transcript*. In that case, the law school may delay an admission decision until it receives your transcript from the school or schools in question.

Above all, remember that avoiding problems at the initial stages of the application process will save you the headache of trying to correct an error at a later stage—when you might have to get in line with several thousand other callers and letter writers requiring assistance from Law Services.

■ *Comply with Deadlines*

Of course, it is especially important to note the law school's application deadline, which is listed in the school's catalog. If you submit your application by the deadline, it is not uncommon for a school to extend its file-completion deadline to accommodate extenuating circumstances. Also, be aware that deadlines for part-time programs may differ from those of full-time programs.

■ *Apply Early*

There are several reasons to take the LSAT and to complete and mail your applications as early as possible after you complete your self-assessment and research. First, you will have more time to fill in any gaps in your application file. Second, you might have more time to evaluate the schools that have accepted you—or to apply to other schools that you had not previously considered. Third, you will reduce the chance of a problem or error in paperwork, which can delay the review of your application. Admission offices are usually flooded with paperwork at the application deadline. Early applications can mean early decisions for some.

If you apply early, it is likely that you will be competing for more first-year seats. On the other hand, a late application may be reviewed more stringently because already-admitted applicants have reduced the number of available seats. **There is never any penalty for applying early.** Consult the sample application schedules shown on pages 70-71 and apply early in the admission cycle of each law school that you select. What is considered early differs from school to school, so inquire at each school where you intend to apply.

■ *Be Honest, Give Full Disclosure, and Follow All Norms of Good Conduct*

Law schools require your language to be your own, and they require your answers to their questions and your personal statement to be direct, honest, and complete. Understand that you are not simply dealing with one office at one school; the choices you make can affect your entire legal career and can become part of a record that follows you wherever you go.

Each year a number of applicants destroy their future careers in law by trying to cut corners in the application process or attempting to press some wrongly perceived advantage. A finding of misconduct can alter permanently any chance for admission to law school. Don't make this mistake in judgment.

Adhering to the norms of good conduct does not simply mean you shouldn't lie or cheat. Some things you may consider perfectly acceptable may be unacceptable to the law schools. Adopt law school rules and standards. Misconduct can include, but is not limited to, the following:

- false statements or omissions of information requested on the Law Services order form, or on other individual law school application forms

- falsification and/or alteration of letters of recommendation, transcript information, school attendance, honors or awards, or employment
- impersonation, cheating, or violation of security procedures during an LSAT administration
- any misleading act or omission, whether intentional or unintentional, on any form or in any statement

When alleged misconduct brings into question the validity of data about a candidate, transmission of the data will be withheld until the matter has been resolved by the Council's Misconduct in the Admission Process Panel. In addition, the Council and Law Services will investigate, at the request of a member law school, instances of alleged misconduct in the admission process not directly related to services provided by Law Services.

As part of these procedures, a three-member panel of the Misconduct in the Admission Process Panel will determine whether misconduct has occurred. If a majority of the panel determines that a preponderance of the evidence shows misconduct, a report of the panel's determination is sent to all law schools to which the applicant has applied or subsequently applies. **These reports are retained indefinitely.** In appropriate cases, state and national bar authorities may also receive notification.

Individual law schools and bar authorities determine what action, if any, they will take in response to a finding of misconduct. Such action may include the following:

- closing of an admission file
- revocation of an offer of admission
- dismissal from law school through a school's internal interdisciplinary channels
- disbarment

Sometimes an act of misconduct can be committed unintentionally; therefore, it is wise to review each step of the admission process thoroughly as you complete it. In fact, it pays to review each step several times. The care and time you take before you submit an application can save you a great deal of trouble down the road.

Many law schools require additional information from the student pertaining to citizenship, legal matters, and any other circumstance that might later prove an obstacle for admission to the bar. Failure to report this information with full disclosure and total accuracy may prove more damaging than the actual nature of the information itself.

Chapter 8

Paying for Law School:
Financial Aid and Debt Management

The cost of attending law school is a figure that includes tuition, fees, books, housing, and other living expenses for the academic year. It can vary significantly from one school to another. Tuition alone can range from a few thousand dollars a year to almost $20,000 per year. After adding in housing, food, books, and personal expenses, the figure may well go beyond $75,000 for a three-year law school education.

Fortunately, there are a number of ways to finance a law school education, but doing so—unless you are independently wealthy—requires thoughtful planning.

There are numerous financial sources from which a student may draw, including family contributions, personal savings, summer and part-time job earnings, scholarships, fellowships, grants, and loans. Most students combine family contributions, summer and/or part-time job income, and loans to pay for law school.

Law school catalogs usually have a section on financial aid. They will list the federal loans available along with institutional aid specific to that particular school or geographical region. In any case, follow the instructions given regarding what forms to obtain and fill out, and what deadlines you must meet. The overall procedure for obtaining financial aid is discussed briefly in the next section, but it is best to follow the guidelines set forth by the individual schools.

You should know, nevertheless, that when considering an applicant for admission, **schools do not consider whether the applicant has filed a financial aid application.** In fact, your financial aid file and your admission file are maintained separately at most law schools. This practice is referred to as "need-blind admission." Do not hesitate to apply for financial aid if you need it when applying for admission to a school that may seem financially out of reach based on your personal resources alone.

Financial Aid Forms and Need Analysis

The first step in applying for financial aid for law school is to request a standardized financial aid form from each law school to which you are applying. You will be required to submit the form to a need-analysis service. The information you provide on your income, savings, assets and other resources will be used to compute how much you and your family should contribute toward your legal education. Many schools also require supplemental information such as copies of annual federal tax returns to verify financial information. Once the analysis is completed, the financial aid officer at the school can determine in addition to your resources what types of aid you will need—such as scholarships, grants, loans, or work-study—to pay your law school expenses.

According to the 1992 reauthorization of the Higher Education Act of 1965, if you are a graduate or professional student in an enrollment period beginning on or after July 1, 1993, you are considered independent. For independent students who are married, financial information is required from the applicant and his or her spouse. Student earnings can have an impact on the equation in a variety of ways. Your base-year income from the previous tax year is the basis of the calculation. If you expect a significant change in your income after you begin law school, you should make sure your financial aid office is informed of this change; for example, if you are employed full time and you plan to stop work entirely, or if you plan to work part time and attend law school on either a full-time or part-time basis. Most law schools also have a summer-savings policy that assumes that a percentage of your summer earnings will be saved and applied to your school-year expenses.

For complete and individualized information on financing your law school education, contact the financial aid office at the individual law school(s) to which you apply. Additional discussion can be found in the *LSAT/LSDAS Registration and Information Book* and *The Official Guide to U.S. Law Schools*, both available from Law Services.

The Package Concept

A financial aid package may include several different types or sources of assistance: grants, scholarships, loans, and work-study programs. Some or all of these may be available **in combination** to bring the cost of attending law school within reach. It's important for law school applicants to understand that law school financial aid packages normally consist of mostly loans and occasionally some grants, in comparison with undergraduate studies, where substantially more grant dollars are available. The amount of aid you receive in each category will depend on your own resources, determined by a need analysis (discussed on pages 82-83) and the financial aid policy of the school.

Scholarships, grants, fellowships. These types of awards, which do not have to be repaid, are given according to need and/or merit. Their availability is quite limited, and they are usually awarded by the law schools themselves, although some limited federal and state programs do exist. The law school's financial aid office can give you more information.

Federal Work-Study (FWS). This federal student aid program allows educational institutions to hire students to work either on- or off-campus for the institution or other eligible employers. Work-study placement is usually awarded to second- and third-year students, because you are expected to concentrate fully on your school work during your first year. Sometimes a student may be able to combine earned income for educational expenses with useful job experience, such as working in a legal aid office.

Loans. Education loans may be awarded directly by the school or through other private agencies. The largest student loan programs are funded or guaranteed by the federal government. Some are awarded on a need basis (see pages 82-83 for more on need analysis), while others are not need-based. Some types of loans will require a credit check. Student loans are usually offered at interest rates lower than consumer loans, and the repayment of principal and interest usually begins after the end of your educational program.

Debt Management

■ *Credit History*

Approximately 75 percent of all law school students borrow money for some or all of their educational costs. If you think you will be among this group of borrowers, it is very important that you have a good credit history. In today's society, most students have already established a credit history through their repayment records as reported by financial institutions and major retail stores to national credit bureaus. Lenders refer to these credit bureau records to determine your credit-worthiness. The credit bureaus report the amounts you borrowed or charged, your outstanding balances, and the promptness by which payments have been made. Failure to pay your financial obligations in a prompt and timely manner will jeopardize your eligibility for some education loans.

Whether you have borrowed or are planning to borrow money for undergraduate school, or make practical use of credit cards during your college years, you must keep in mind that your ability to borrow money for law school—as well as to secure future credit for a home, car, or other loans—depends on how well you have managed the payment of your credit obligations all along the way.

If you have been denied credit in the past—or if you even suspect a problem with your credit history—it is wise to get a copy of your credit report. Usually, you can obtain it from a credit bureau in your area. Contact the bureau in writing, giving your name, address, and social security number. You can expect to pay a nominal fee, unless you have been denied credit recently, in which case the report may be free. Review your report carefully and clear up any problems you can. Keep in mind that it takes time—possibly months—to clear up errors or other problems, so do not wait until the last minute.

▪ Loan Default or Delinquency

These two terms are often confused: **delinquency** occurs when you have begun repayment on a loan or other obligation and have missed one or more payment dates; **default** generally occurs when a delinquency goes beyond 150-180 days. Delinquencies appear on credit records and may hinder you from qualifying for an education loan that requires a credit check. Defaults are even more serious and are likely to prevent you from successfully applying for federal financial aid as well as disqualify you for most other educational loans. If you are in a default status, you must take steps to change your status if you wish to apply for a federally guaranteed loan for law school. Contact the servicer of your loan(s) for more information on this subject.

▪ Planning Ahead: A Realistic Look at the Future

We've said that assessing your credit history before you begin applying for loans can save you undue time and can minimize stress by allowing you to straighten out any problems in advance. Similarly, realistically assessing your imagined future, specifically your career and salary expectations, before applying for a loan will help you determine just how much money you will be able to pay back, and how soon you can retire your educational debt once you complete law school. Your income after law school is an important factor in determining what constitutes manageable payments on your education loans. Although it may be difficult to predict what kind of job you will get (or want) after law school, or exactly what kind of salary you will receive, it is important that you make some assessment of your goals for the purpose of sound debt management. In addition to assessing expected income—and it is essential that you be realistic when you do so—you must also evaluate your projected lifestyle objectives. You will need to create a pragmatic picture of how much you can afford to pay back on a monthly basis and maintain the lifestyle that you desire. You may have to adjust your thinking about how quickly you can pay your loans back, or how much money you can afford to borrow, or just how extravagantly you can expect to live in the years following graduation from law school.

■ *Repayment of Your Loan*

Your education loan debts represent a serious financial commitment that must be repaid. A default on any loan engenders serious consequences, including possible legal action against you by the lender and/or the government.

There are alternatives available to you to lessen the burden of repayment following law school, including the federal loan consolidation program. A growing number of law schools are developing loan forgiveness programs for graduates who enter low-paying public service jobs. The financial aid office at your law school can advise you about repayment issues.

Chapter 9

The Admission Process: What You Need to Know

After you have done everything you possibly can to prepare yourself—you've carefully examined your own motivation in going to law school; you've assessed first yourself and then the schools; you've selected a handful of schools to which you have now applied for admission, and perhaps for financial aid as well (see Chapter 8)—there is nothing to do but sit back and wait for a response.

It helps, however, to know just what is going on back there in the admission office, where some nameless person is reading your application file along with the files of hundreds or perhaps thousands of others. What is he or she thinking? How will these readers arrive at a decision? Who are these people, anyway?

Who Makes Admission Decisions?

Each school handles the admission process just a bit differently. At many schools the director of admission is a nonfaculty member who represents the admission office in an administrative capacity. In such cases, the director of admission may not be a voting member of the admission committee. In other cases, the director of admission can automatically admit candidates with exceptional credentials (particularly the admission index) at his or her discretion. Less commonly, the director of admission is authorized to deny applicants whose credentials clearly fall below the standards of the law school.

Admission-committee members typically consist of law school faculty. However, at many institutions, law students serve either in an advisory capacity or as actual voting members. At least one law school gives applicants the option of having their file reviewed by student committee members (candidates check a box on their application form). If you want to know if student personnel will be reviewing your application, contact the admission office of the schools to which you are applying.

When Are Decisions Made?

Again, the answer varies from school to school. Most law school admission decisions are made sometime between December and

June. The law schools that receive the largest number of applications start making decisions earlier than those that receive fewer applications, although there are some exceptions.

Some admission committees begin to evaluate files on a rolling-admission basis, reviewing batches of completed files as soon as they receive them, some as early as October. Some may review your file as soon as they have received your completed LSDAS report. You can see, then, why it is important that you submit your letters of recommendation and any other supporting materials as early as possible.

If your file is reviewed on a rolling-admission basis, you may be notified shortly after a decision has been made. Schools that do not use a rolling-admission process usually wait until early April to announce all their decisions at once.

Early decision. A small number of schools offer early decision admission programs. By applying through the early decision program, you are telling a particular school it is your first choice and, if you accept its offer of admission, you will withdraw your applications from all other law schools and attend that school. Early decision offers are made early in the year and can include a demand for a deposit prior to the April 1 deadline often observed for regular admission. The advantage of such programs is that, with the admission process behind you, you can begin planning for law school because you know where you will attend. If you don't get admitted through early decision, you continue in the regular admission process.

Making inquiries about your application. In general, you should inquire about the status of your application only if 1) the law school has not notified you that your application is complete and in the process of being reviewed; 2) you have not received a decision within a reasonable time of such a notification; or 3) you have been admitted to another law school that requires a deposit fairly soon. In such cases, a discreet inquiry about your application is acceptable. Some schools specifically request that inquiries be made only in writing. Check the law school's catalog.

Finally, although all admission offices do try to notify applicants as promptly as possible, the decision-making process can be very complex. In the next section, we take a look at how decisions are made.

How Decisions Are Made

■ *Criteria*

We have already discussed the various elements in your application as they relate to maximizing your chances of admission. Law schools do not all make admission decisions in exactly the same manner, and they do not all require the same information. Nevertheless, let us review here the elements we have discussed in different places in this book, and list them here as specific criteria that law schools consider when making admission decisions:

- Your Law School Admission Test score
- Your undergraduate grade-point average and transcript
- Your undergraduate course of study
- Graduate study, if any
- The college you attended
- Improvement in your grades and grade distribution
- Your college activities, both curricular and extracurricular
- Your minority status
- Your moral character and personality
- Your letters of recommendation
- Your written essay and/or personal interview
- Significant activities since you graduated from college, such as work experience
- Your state of residency
- Your motivation to study and reasons for deciding to study law
- Finally, anything else from your file that might make a member of the admission committee sit up and take notice.

Many prospective law students believe that the LSAT and GPA scores seal their fate. Although some law school admission officers share that view, others point out that so many good applicants have the same range of grades and LSAT scores that it's impossible to narrow the field using these two criteria alone.

The Law School Admission Council's *Statement of Good Admission Practices* has this to say about LSAT scores and the GPA, respectively:

LSAT scores provide at best a partial measure of an applicant's ability and should be considered in relation to the total range of information about a prospective law student. [It] should be used as only one of several criteria for evaluation and should not be given undue weight. ...

Undergraduate grades are a significant indicator of significant success in law school. ... There are, of course, measures of intellectual ability other than cumulative grade-point average. Unusual creativity, exceptional research skills, analytical prowess, and other factors may not be reflected on a candidate's college transcript.

■ *Candidate Pools*

Admissions officers are also looking to put together an interesting group of people who will bring with them different perspectives. According to the Law School Admission Council:

... a law school's institutional admission policies may result in a preference for certain applicants. Each law school's admission policies should be adequately disclosed to all prospective applicants at the outset of the admission process.

At the same time, the Council notes that:

Admission of applicants from a wide variety of academic, cultural, ethnic, and racial backgrounds, and the resulting diversity, enhances and enriches the educational experiences of all students and faculty.

It's fair to assume that all ABA-approved law schools abide by the Council's *Statement of Good Admission Practices*. For example, the admission policy of one distinguished law school regarding minority and disabled applicants states as follows:

An applicant's racial or cultural minority background may be considered a 'plus' if he or she is a member of a group which has not had a fair opportunity to develop its potential achievement and which lacks adequate representation within the legal profession.

Physical and other disability should be taken into consideration when there is sufficient evidence to establish that the disability has affected academic predictors.

How Readers Arrive at Decisions

Again, different schools arrive at their final decisions through different avenues, but, in most cases, candidates who are likely to be admitted or likely to be denied are separated out fairly quickly. For the sake of our discussion, we might refer to three groups: the admits, the rejects, and—the largest group—the holds (or the we're-not-certain-yet group). Although a strong admission index (see pages 72-73) may place a candidate into a "probably admit" category, some schools with a rolling-admission policy may adjust the index up or down, depending on the number of applications they receive and the quality of the applicants.

At some schools, the full admission committee may not examine all the files, but will see only those in the middle-range group. Sometimes it may be the dean who does this initial sorting; sometimes it may be an administrator. Applicants with credentials just below the top often are reviewed more extensively by the full admission committee. Members may vote on these files individually, or they may reach a consensus in conference. In addition to making further decisions on this group about whether to admit or to deny admission, some files may be put into one of two additional categories: hold or waiting list.

Hold status. Candidates placed into this category are those for whom the admission committee is unable to make a clear-cut decision after the first round of decisions is made, defined by the time when seat deposits are required. Applicants whose files are on hold still have a chance to be admitted; there are still seats to fill in the first-year class. According to one law school bulletin, an applicant is placed in the hold group if he or she "does not quite meet the standards of those currently being admitted, but has strong qualifications that indicate possible admission later in the season." Some schools notify an applicant of their hold status; others do not. Furthermore, the committee can continue to put a candidate's file on hold after the second or third round of decisions.

Waiting list. If you are placed on the waiting list, on the other hand, you are notified of this status after the first-year seats have been filled. Your chance of admission, therefore, is influenced by the volume of applications nationwide. Generally speaking, the lower the volume, the better your chances. In a "seller's market," where there are many more applicants than available seats, the school is less likely to turn to its waiting list. On the other hand, when applications are down, more candidates tend to enroll in their first-choice schools, leaving empty seats in the other schools that accepted them. In those cases, law schools turn to their waiting lists.

In most cases, law schools will tell you whether you've been placed on a waiting list. By contacting a law school directly, you may be able to get an idea of your chances for admission. First, ask the admission office how many students have been placed on the waiting list. If you can get that information, try to find out your ranking, as well as the number of students admitted from the waiting list in the past two or three years.

Although the Law School Admission Council advises law schools to "maintain a waiting list of reasonable length and only for a reasonable length of time," schools sometimes admit candidates as late as the week classes begin.

Postadmission Considerations

Many law schools use seat deposits to help keep track of their incoming classes. A school may require an initial acceptance fee of $100, which is credited to your first-term tuition if you actually register at the school. If you decline the offer of admission after you've paid your deposit, a portion of the money may be refunded, depending on the date you actually decline the offer. Some schools refund none of the deposit. The following passage describes the official position of the Law School Admission Council:

> Except under early decision plans, law schools should permit applicants to choose, without penalty, among offers of admission and financial aid until April 1. Admitted applicants who have submitted a timely financial aid application should not be required to commit to enroll until notified of financial awards that are within control of the law school. … Every accepted applicant should be free to deal with all law schools

and to accept an offer from one of them even though a
deposit has been paid to another school.

For more complete information on the process of applying for
financial aid, see Chapter 8.

■ *Notify Law Schools*

You can help take some of the complexity out of the admission
process with one simple act of courtesy: once you have decided
where to enroll, promptly notify any other schools that have
accepted or wait-listed you. Your consideration will pay off in two
ways: first, you'll be helping a good wait-listed student get into
law school; second, by not tying up more than one seat, you'll help
make the admission process work more efficiently for everyone.

■ *Don't Just Attend Any Law School*

What if you suddenly develop second thoughts about the one law
school that accepts you? You don't have to settle for the wrong
school just because it sends you an acceptance letter. Think about
the alternatives. What if you postponed your legal education for a
year? What if you rethought your application strategies and came
up with a new list of schools to which you could apply? You're
likely to be happier—both in the long and short run—if you attend
a law school that is right for you.

Chapter 10

After Law School: Taking the Bar Exam and Finding a Job

The Bar Exam

Admission to law school and admission to the bar are two very different matters; with very few exceptions, graduation from the former in no way automatically insures admission to the latter.

Between your last celebratory graduation party and your first job looms the bar exam and, as with the LSAT, preparation will enhance your performance.

Each state's bar exam tests your mastery of basic legal concepts and your knowledge of the law of that state. Many states will use the Multi-State Bar Exam (MBE) as one part of their comprehensive examination. The MBE is a standardized, multiple-choice test that can be used in any jurisdiction because it tests basic legal concepts as they might occur in any law of any state. The bar exam will also include essay questions, and some states require a multiple-choice ethics exam called the Multi-State Professional Responsibility Exam (MPRE).

As we pointed out in Chapter 6, ABA-approved law schools do not emphasize state-specific law in the approved curriculum, although individual curricula may offer specific electives for second- and third-year students that focus on a state's laws. Therefore, it is standard practice for candidates to rely primarily on a review course to prepare them for this aspect of the test. The bar review courses are usually offered by private companies located in various states and are taught by law school professors and practicing attorneys. The courses are only a few weeks in length and are given prior to each bar exam.

Finding Legal Employment

The supply and demand for lawyers varies by geography, by practice area, and over time. Your ability to find a job will depend not only on such external factors as conditions in the legal profession and in the economy in general, but also on how well you have done in law school, how motivated you are, what your job expectations are, and how flexible those expectations are. Realistically, you should give some thought to your career expectations after law school even before you apply.

■ *Career Satisfaction*

A job-search strategy requires careful self-assessment in much the same way as a school-search strategy does. A legal career should meet the interests, abilities, capacities, and priorities of the individual lawyer. Career satisfaction is a result of doing what you like to do, and being continually challenged by it. It is up to you to determine what skills you are comfortable using, and to discern which skills are required in the specialties or types of practice you are considering.

One of the reasons many law students find the legal job search a source of frustration is that so many are competing in a very small, narrowly defined job market. Review Chapter 2, in which we describe a range of opportunities that exist for law school graduates. Despite the fact that students enter law school from a wide variety of backgrounds, many arrive—in the course of their law school education—at the common goal of working for a large or medium-sized law practice in a major metropolitan area for which competition is quite stiff, not in the least because the salaries are at the higher end of the scale. Clearly, however, not everyone has the qualifications necessary to secure one of these positions; moreover, there are fewer such positions than applicants even among those who **are** qualified. Perhaps more important, not everyone has the temperament for this kind of work. Students would do well to remember that this is only one of many avenues open to them after law school and, like any option, it has its advantages and disadvantages.

As a law school graduate, you should expand your view to include other areas of traditional practice—small law firms, government agencies, corporate legal departments, public interest organizations, solo practice—and explore new developments in law as well. Keep in mind also that the skills you learned in law school—analytical reasoning, writing, and oral advocacy—can be transferred to a host of nontraditional career options as well (see pages 22-23).

■ *Career Services*

Earlier, we listed the law school career office as one factor in initially selecting a school that meets your needs. While you are in law school, the career services office can be a valuable source of information on summer jobs and internships—once you get beyond your first year—as well as on jobs after you graduate. Therefore, you should familiarize yourself with this office as soon as you become involved with a law school.

Career offices vary in what services they offer. Staff may be available to read drafts of students' résumés and cover letters, to discuss job-search strategies, to help identify prospective employers, and sometimes to lead students through mock interviews. Some schools even videotape the mock interviews to help identify and solve interviewing problems. Here again you must identify your own needs, investigate carefully the schools that interest you, and find those that match your requirements.

Take advantage of any programs and workshops offered by your placement office. Place your name on file in the office. You never know when something will come up that will be the perfect match for you. It may happen after you leave school, so be sure to maintain contact with the staff.

■ *Job Recruitment at Law School*

Students at highly competitive schools, especially those who are enjoying academic success, are typically (during periods of economic growth) courted by large law firms which send representatives out to the schools to interview them. This recruitment initially begins during the law student's second or third year, when firms recruit students for internships or summer jobs. This process occurs regionally as well. But not every student is courted; most have to do the courting themselves. Furthermore, not all firms have the resources to actively recruit, and depend instead on word-of-mouth and the résumés that come in over the transom. You should begin early to search out job possibilities on your own—**while** you're in law school, not after you're finished. Develop your own contacts; make maximum use of the resources of your placement office; do research about other areas of the country and other options for work besides the most visible law firms.

National Association for Law Placement (NALP)

This nonprofit, educational organization composed of ABA-approved law schools and about 750 legal employers of all sizes (including law firms, government and public interest organizations, corporations, and accounting firms) promotes career development for lawyers and aims to improve the process by which those careers are implemented. The association provides a national forum for the exchange of information, promotes career planning and placement, and provides counseling, among other functions. It also publishes several reference sources you may find useful: a guide to law schools, including placement profiles of each member school; an employment report and salary survey (which is summarized in *The Official Guide to U.S. Law Schools* each year); a directory of employers, and a publication that offers information on nontraditional legal employment.

Chapter 11

Getting Started

This book began with the premise that its readers are individuals who come to law from a multiplicity of directions and with varying degrees of commitment to law as a career. Some of you may have considered a career in law in a fleeting way; others of you have been planning your life in the law for quite some time. No matter how uncertain or how clear you are with respect to your own goals, we hope we have posed some important questions for you to consider. We hope too that we have been able to shed some light on what lawyering and law school are really about.

The chapters in this book have outlined various important aspects of thinking about law school, from your self-assessment and information gathering through your selection and application to the law schools themselves. Although each chapter turned the lens on a particular area of concern, the one resounding theme throughout *Law as a Career: A Practical Guide* has been this: you must find the law school or schools that seem right for you.

You begin by gathering the necessary information, making a plan, and putting your plan into action. You've already taken one important step in reading this book. The next step is to gather information: talk to prelaw advisors, look through *The Official Guide to U.S. Law Schools*, contact law schools, and read law school catalogs. Consult other Law Services publications. Call and visit law schools. Attend a Law School Forum. Finally, complete the necessary registration and application forms carefully and methodically.

Use the information within these pages to challenge your assumptions about law school. Put aside the labels; don't apply to a school because you've heard it's good or your family wants you to attend. Don't minimize your chances for admission; there are 191 law schools in the United States and Canada. Among them you will find one or more law schools that are right for you. You must, however, realistically evaluate your credentials and apply to those schools that best meet your needs and abilities.

As you know by now, the search we have outlined can be extremely challenging. However, by taking the time to develop and implement an effective strategy, you can make the process an exciting and rewarding one. Take the next step now; start working on your plan. Good luck!

Appendix A

Differences between ABA-approved and Non-ABA-approved Law Schools

Approved Law Schools

ABA-approved schools. Currently, 176 United States law schools granting the J.D. degree have been approved by the American Bar Association (ABA), that is, they comply with the ABA Standards for Approval of Law Schools. A degree from an ABA-approved school meets the minimum legal educational requirement of all states and the District of Columbia, Puerto Rico, the U.S. Virgin Islands, and Guam. Such a degree entitles a student to take state bar examinations and to practice law in the state or states where he or she is licensed.

Schools with provisional ABA approval. The initial process for a law school seeking approval by the ABA is an application for provisional approval. The ABA standards define that the school "substantially complies with the [ABA] Standards and gives assurances that it will be in full compliance with the Standards within three years after receiving provisional approval." A law school can be granted full approval after having been provisionally approved for at least two years. Graduating from a school with provisional ABA accreditation entitles the student "to the same recognition accorded to students and graduates of fully approved schools." The ABA recognizes the student as a graduate of a fully approved law school even if the school's approval rating had been rescinded during the student's matriculation.

State-approved schools. Graduates of state-approved law schools usually are certified only in the state in which they received their degree. They cannot take the bar examination or practice law anywhere else.

Unapproved Schools

If your credentials for admission to law school are not what they should be, alternatives such as unapproved law schools, may begin to look attractive. There are basically three types of unapproved law schools, which are described below. Each of these options has specific risks and limitations.

■ *New Schools*

There are some schools that have not been operating long enough to obtain ABA approval—or are not currently satisfying ABA standards. Here are some guidelines to help you assess the risks involved in choosing such a school:

- Have at least some of the administration and faculty been recruited from ABA-approved law schools?
- Examine the school's financial commitment and resources. Are there ample classrooms, library space, and other facilities needed to run a program of high quality?
- Is the law school part of an established university or, better still, part of a state university? This is an important point, because universities supported by state funding tend to be stable institutions. Independent schools are not automatically suspect, but university affiliation signals the availability of adequate resources and support.
- Has the school made a public statement that it has applied or will apply for ABA approval? By putting its reputation on the line, a school is apt to work especially hard to meet ABA standards.

It may take some work but you can compare the unapproved law schools to their ABA-approved counterparts on such factors as library holdings, range of courses offered, faculty-student ratio, and other criteria discussed earlier in this book. Also, you may telephone the office of the ABA's Consultant on Legal Education at 317.264.8340 to learn if the school has applied for ABA approval. [Special thanks are due to the ABA Office of the Consultant for providing this source of information for the reader.]

■ *Schools That Have Not Been—And Will Not Be—Approved*

Some states permit graduates of unapproved law schools to take the bar examination or to be admitted reciprocally but most do not. Before you apply or enroll in any school, carefully consider the limitations that these unapproved programs impose, such as limiting practice to the state in which the school is located. About 70 percent of the unapproved law schools in the United States are in the state of California.

Foreign law schools. Think twice before attending a foreign law school if you plan to practice law in the United States. After graduating, you probably will still need at least one full year of legal study in the U.S. to be eligible to take the bar. If you feel you must attend a foreign law school, find out exactly what you will have to do to be admitted to a state bar when you return. Of course, there are a few foreign study opportunities you would almost never pass up: a Rhodes scholarship or law study at Oxford or Cambridge are two examples. For more information on the subject of foreign law schools and U.S. bar exams, consult the ABA's *Comprehensive Guide to Bar Admission Requirements.*

■ *Other Strategies Not Recommended*

Reading the law. Is it possible to learn the law exclusively through "on the job training," that is, by apprenticing yourself to office study? Not really, even though the practice was common in frontier America. Today, only eight states retain the reading-law concept, and they have restrictive regulations. The number of such students admitted to practice is extremely low. Almost as rare are state provisions that sanction law school study that is supplemented by office study.

Law by mail. "You can learn law in your spare time, double your income, and become a respected member of your community," says the ad for correspondence law study. What the ad does not say is that you cannot become a member of the bar association in most states. The Council of the Section of Legal Education and Admissions to the Bar of the ABA has this to say on the subject of correspondence schools: "The American Bar Association expressly disapproves of correspondence law courses as a means of preparation for bar examination and for practice. Correspondence law school graduates may take the bar examination only in California and even there only under special circumstances." Some prospective law students actually have enrolled in law-by-mail as a preparation for formal law school education. The strategy has no merit.

Conclusion

Should you think about attending a law school that has no chance of ever obtaining ABA approval? In a word, no. However, if you are absolutely determined to go to law school one way or another, you must ask yourself if your degree will have any practical value. Will it allow you to take a bar examination and give you the chance to be admitted to the practice of law? If so, will you be adequately prepared for a legal career, or will you be forced into nonlegal jobs for which your training was not even necessary? It is **imperative** that you learn the school's bar examination passage rate and the percentage of graduates who find jobs. You may be one of the few who attend an unapproved law school, pass the bar, and benefit from a rewarding career, but you will be defying the odds all the way.

Appendix B

U.S. Law Schools Approved by the American Bar Association

The following list of ABA-approved law schools was accurate as of the publication of this book. For the most up-to-date information about individual schools, see the latest edition of *The Official Guide to U.S. Law Schools.*

University of Akron
School of Law
Akron, OH 44325-2901

University of Alabama
School of Law
101 Paul Bryant Drive
Tuscaloosa, AL 35487

Albany Law School
of Union University
80 New Scotland Avenue
Albany, NY 12208

American University
Washington College of Law
4400 Massachusetts
Avenue, N.W.
Washington, DC 20016

University of Arizona
College of Law
Tucson, AZ 85721

Arizona State University
College of Law
Tempe, AZ 85287-7906

University of
Arkansas—Fayetteville
School of Law
Fayetteville, AR 72701

University of Arkansas—
Little Rock
School of Law
1201 McAlmont
Little Rock, AR 72202-5142

University of Baltimore
School of Law
1420 North Charles Street
Baltimore, MD 21201

Baylor University
School of Law
P.O. Box 97288
Waco, TX 76798-7288

Boston College
Law School
885 Centre Street
Newton, MA 02159

Boston University
School of Law
765 Commonwealth Avenue
Boston, MA 02215

Bridgeport School of Law
at Quinnipiac College
303 University Avenue
Bridgeport, CT 06604

Brigham Young University
J. Reuben Clark Law School
340 JRCB
Provo, UT 84602

Brooklyn Law School
250 Joralemon Street
Brooklyn, NY 11201

University of California—
Berkeley
School of Law
220 Boalt Hall
Berkeley, CA 94720

University of California—Davis
School of Law
King Hall
Davis, CA 95616-5201

University of California
Hastings College of Law
200 McAllister Street
San Francisco, CA 94102

University of California—
Los Angeles
School of Law
71 Dodd Hall
405 Hilgard Avenue
Los Angeles, CA 90024-1445

California Western
School of Law
350 Cedar Street
San Diego, CA 92101

Campbell University
School of Law
Box 158
Buies Creek, NC 27506

Capital University
Law School
665 South High Street
Columbus, OH 43215

Benjamin N. Cardozo
School of Law
Yeshiva University
55 Fifth Avenue
New York, NY 10003

Case Western Reserve University
School of Law
11075 East Boulevard
Cleveland, OH 44106

Catholic University
of America
School of Law
Washington, DC 20064

Catholic University of
Puerto Rico
School of Law
Ponce, PR 00732

Chicago-Kent Law School
Illinois Institute of Technology
565 West Adams Street
Chicago, IL 60661-3691

University of Chicago
Law School
1111 East 60th Street
Chicago, IL 60637

University of Cincinnati
College of Law
M.L. 40
Cincinnati, OH 45221

Cleveland State University
Cleveland-Marshall
College of Law
Cleveland, OH 44115

University of Colorado
School of Law
Campus Box 403
Boulder, CO 80309-0403

Columbia University
School of Law
435 West 116th Street
New York, NY 10027

University of Connecticut
School of Law
55 Elizabeth Street
Hartford, CT 06105-2296

Cornell Law School
College Avenue
240 Myron Taylor Hall
Ithaca, NY 14853-4901

Creighton University
School of Law
2133 California Street
Omaha, NE 68178-0340

University of Dayton
School of Law
300 College Park
Dayton, OH 45469-1320

University of Denver
College of Law
7039 East 18th Street
Denver, CO 80220

DePaul University
College of Law
25 East Jackson Boulevard
Chicago, IL 60604

University of Detroit Mercy
School of Law
651 East Jefferson Avenue
Detroit, MI 48226

Detroit College of Law
130 East Elizabeth Street
Detroit, MI 48201

Dickinson School of Law
150 South College Street
Carlisle, PA 17013

District of Columbia
School of Law
719 13th Street NW
Washington, DC 20005

Drake University
Law School
Cartwright Hall
27th & Carpenter
Des Moines, IA 50311

Duke University
School of Law
University Tower
3101 Petty Road
Suite 207
Durham, NC 27706

Duquesne University
School of Law
900 Locust Street
Pittsburgh, PA 15282

Emory University
School of Law
Gambrell Hall
Atlanta, GA 30322

University of Florida
College of Law
164 Holland Hall
Gainesville, FL 32611

Florida State University
College of Law
425 W. Jefferson Street
Tallahassee, FL 32306-1034

Fordham University
School of Law
140 West 62nd Street
New York, NY 10023

Franklin Pierce
Law Center
2 White Street
Concord, NH 03301

George Mason University
School of Law
3401 North Fairfax Drive
Arlington, VA 22201-4498

George Washington University
National Law Center
Stockton Hall, Room 101
Washington, DC 20052

Georgetown University
Law Center
600 New Jersey Avenue, N.W.
Washington, DC 20001

University of Georgia
School of Law
Athens, GA 30602

Georgia State University
College of Law
University Plaza
Atlanta, GA 30303-3092

Golden Gate University
School of Law
536 Mission Street
San Francisco, CA 94105

Gonzaga University
School of Law
Box 3528
Spokane, WA 99220

Hamline University
School of Law
1536 Hewitt Avenue
St. Paul, MN 55104

Harvard Law School
1563 Massachusetts Avenue
Cambridge, MA 02138

University of Hawaii
William S. Richardson
School of Law
2515 Dole Street
Honolulu, HI 96822

Hofstra University
School of Law
1000 Fulton Avenue
Hempstead, NY 11550

University of Houston
Law Center
4800 Calhoun
Houston, TX 77204-6391

Howard University
School of Law
2900 Van Ness Street, N.W.
Washington, DC 20008

University of Idaho
College of Law
Moscow, ID 83843

University of Illinois
College of Law
504 East Pennsylvania
Champaign, IL 61820

Indiana University—
Bloomington
School of Law
Bloomington, IN 47405

Indiana University—
Indianapolis
School of Law
735 West New York Street
Indianapolis, IN 46202

Inter American University
School of Law
P.O. Box 8897
Santurce, PR 00910

University of Iowa
College of Law
276 Boyd Law Building
Melrose at Byington Streets
Iowa City, IA 52242

John Marshall Law School
315 South Plymouth Court
Chicago, IL 60604

University of Kansas
School of Law
Lawrence, KS 66045

University of Kentucky
College of Law
Lexington, KY 40506-0048

Lewis and Clark College
Northwestern School of Law
10015 Terwilliger Boulevard
Portland, OR 97219

Louisiana State University
Paul M. Hebert Law Center
Baton Rouge, LA 70803

University of Louisville
School of Law
Belknap Campus
Louisville, KY 40292

Loyola Law School—
Los Angeles
1441 West Olympic Boulevard
Box 15019
Los Angeles, CA 90015-3980

Loyola University—Chicago
School of Law
One East Delaware, Suite 300
Chicago, IL 60611

Loyola University—New Orleans
School of Law
7214 St. Charles Avenue, Box 904
New Orleans, LA 70118

University of Maine
School of Law
246 Deering Avenue
Portland, ME 04102

Marquette University
Law School
1103 West Wisconsin Avenue
Milwaukee, WI 53233

University of Maryland
School of Law
500 West Baltimore Street
Baltimore, MD 21201

McGeorge School of Law
University of the Pacific
3200 Fifth Avenue
Sacramento, CA 95817

Memphis State University
Cecil C. Humphreys
School of Law
Memphis, TN 38152

Mercer University
Walter F. George
School of Law
1021 Georgia Avenue
Macon, GA 31201-6709

University of Miami
School of Law
P. O. Box 248087
Coral Gables, FL 33124-8087

University of Michigan
Law School
625 South State Street,
Room 320
Ann Arbor, MI 48109-1215

University of Minnesota
Law School
229 19th Avenue South
Minneapolis, MN 55455

University of Mississippi
School of Law
University, MS 38677

Mississippi College
School of Law
151 East Griffith Street
Jackson, MS 39201

University of
Missouri—Columbia
School of Law
Law Building
Columbia, MO 65211

University of Missouri—
Kansas City
School of Law
5100 Rockhill Road
Kansas City, MO 64110

University of Montana
School of Law
Missoula, MT 59812

University of Nebraska
College of Law
42nd & Fair Streets
Lincoln, NE 68583-0902

New England School of Law
154 Stuart Street
Boston, MA 02116

University of New Mexico
School of Law
1117 Stanford Drive, N.E.
Albuquerque, NM 87131

CUNY Law School
at Queens College
65-21 Main Street
Flushing, NY 11367

SUNY at Buffalo
School of Law
312 O'Brien Hall
Buffalo, NY 14260

New York Law School
57 Worth Street
New York, NY 10013

New York University
School of Law
40 Washington Square South
New York, NY 10012

University of North Carolina
School of Law
CB 3380
Chapel Hill, NC 27599-3380

North Carolina Central
University
School of Law
1512 South Alston Avenue
Durham, NC 27707

University of North Dakota
School of Law
P.O. Box 9003
Grand Forks, ND 58202

Northeastern University
School of Law
400 Huntington Avenue
Boston, MA 02115

Northern Illinois University
College of Law
DeKalb, IL 60115

Northern Kentucky University
Salmon P. Chase
College of Law
Nunn Hall , Room 530
Highland Heights, KY
41099-6031

Northwestern University
School of Law
357 East Chicago Avenue
Chicago, IL 60611

Notre Dame Law School
Notre Dame, IN 46556

Nova University
Shepard Broad Law Center
3305 College Avenue
Fort Lauderdale, FL 33314

Ohio Northern University
Pettit College of Law
525 S. Main Street
Ada, OH 45810

Ohio State University
College of Law
1659 North High Street
Columbus, OH 43210

University of Oklahoma
Law Center
300 Timberdell Road
Norman, OK 73019

Oklahoma City University
Law School
P.O. Box 61310
Oklahoma City, OK 73146-1310

University of Oregon
School of Law
1101 Kincaid Street
Eugene, OR 97403

Pace University
School of Law
78 North Broadway
White Plains, NY 10603

University of Pennsylvania
Law School
3400 Chestnut Street
Philadelphia, PA 19104

Pepperdine University
School of Law
24255 Pacific Coast Highway
Malibu, CA 90263

University of Pittsburgh
School of Law
3900 Forbes Avenue
Pittsburgh, PA 15260

University of Puerto Rico
School of Law
Rio Pedras, PR 00931

University of Puget Sound
School of Law
950 Broadway Plaza
Tacoma, WA 98402

Regent University
School of Law
1000 Centerville Turnpike
Virginia Beach, VA 23464

University of Richmond
T.C. Williams School of Law
University of Richmond,
VA 23173

Rutgers University—Camden
School of Law
P.O. Box 93650
Camden, NJ 08101-3650

Rutgers University—Newark
School of Law
15 Washington Street
Newark, NJ 07102

St. John's University
School of Law
Fromkes Hall
Grand Central & Utopia Parkways
Jamaica, NY 11439

St. Louis University
School of Law
3700 Lindell Boulevard
St. Louis, MO 63108

St. Mary's University of
San Antonio
School of Law
One Camino Santa Maria
San Antonio, TX 78228-8601

St. Thomas University
School of Law
16400 N.W. 32nd Avenue
Miami, FL 33054

Cumberland School of Law
Samford University
800 Lakeshore Drive
Birmingham, AL 35229

University of San Diego
School of Law
5998 Alcala Park
San Diego, CA 92110

University of San Francisco
School of Law
2199 Fullton Street
San Francisco, CA 94117-1080

Santa Clara University
School of Law
Santa Clara, CA 95053

Seton Hall University
School of Law
One Newark Center
Newark, NJ 07102-5210

University of South Carolina
School of Law
Main & Green Streets
Columbia, SC 29208

University of South Dakota
School of Law
414 East Clark Street
Vermillion, SD 57069-2390

South Texas College of Law
1303 San Jacinto
Houston, TX 77002-7006

University of Southern
California
Law Center
University Park MC 0071
Los Angeles, CA 90089-0071

Southern Illinois University
School of Law
Carbondale, IL 62901

Southern Methodist University
School of Law
3315 Daniel Avenue
Dallas, TX 75275-0116

Southern University
Law Center
P.O. Box 9294
Baton Rouge, LA 70813

Southwestern University
School of Law
675 South Westmoreland Avenue
Los Angeles, CA 90005-3992

Stanford Law School
Stanford, CA 94305

Stetson University
College of Law
1401 61st Street South
St. Petersburg, FL 33707

Suffolk University
Law School
41 Temple Street
Boston, MA 02114

Syracuse University
College of Law
Syracuse, NY 13244-1030

Temple University
School of Law
1719 North Broad Street,
Klein Hall, Room 516
Philadelphia, PA 19122

University of Tennessee
College of Law
1505 West Cumberland
Avenue
Knoxville, TN 37996-1800

University of Texas
School of Law
727 East 26th Street
Austin, TX 78705

Texas Southern University
Thurgood Marshall
School of Law
3100 Cleburne Avenue
Houston, TX 77004

Texas Tech University
School of Law
Lubbock, TX 79409

Thomas M. Cooley
Law School
507 South Grand Avenue
Lansing, MI 48901

University of Toledo
College of Law
Toledo, OH 43606

Touro College
Jacob D. Fuchsberg Law Center
300 Nassau Road
Huntington, NY 11743

Tulane University
School of Law
6801 Freret Street
New Orleans, LA 70118

University of Tulsa
College of Law
3120 East Fourth Place
Tulsa, OK 74104

University of Utah
College of Law
101 Law Building
Salt Lake City, UT 84112

Valparaiso University
School of Law
Valparaiso, IN 46383

Vanderbilt University
School of Law
21st Avenue, South
Nashville, TN 37240

Vermont Law School
P.O. Box 96
South Royalton, VT 05068

Villanova University
School of Law
Villanova, PA 19085

University of Virginia
School of Law
North Grounds
Charlottesville, VA 22901

Wake Forest University
School of Law
Corner Wingate Drive &
Carsinell Drive
Winston-Salem, NC 27109

Washburn University
School of Law
Topeka, KS 66621

University of Washington
School of Law
1100 N.E. Campus Parkway
JB-20
Seattle, WA 98105

Washington and Lee University
School of Law
Lewis Hall
Lexington, VA 24450

Washington University
School of Law
One Brookings Drive
Campus Box 1120
St. Louis, MO 63130

Wayne State University
Law School
468 West Ferry
Detroit, MI 48202

West Virginia University
College of Law
P.O. Box 6130
Morgantown, WV 26506

Western New England College
School of Law
1215 Wilbraham Road
Springfield, MA 01119-9989

Whittier College
School of Law
5353 West Third Street
Los Angeles, CA 90020

Widener University
School of Law
P.O. Box 7474, Concord Pike
Wilmington, DE 19803

Willamette University
College of Law
245 Winter Street, S.E.
Salem, OR 97301

College of William and Mary
Marshall-Wythe School of Law
Williamsburg, VA 23185

William Mitchell
College of Law
875 Summit Avenue
St. Paul, MN 55105

University of Wisconsin
Law School
Madison, WI 53706

University of Wyoming
College of Law
University Station
P.O. Box 3035
Laramie, WY 82071-3035

Yale Law School
127 Wall Steet
Drawer 401A, Yale Station
New Haven, CT 06520

Appendix C

Canadian Member Law Schools

The following list was accurate as of the publication of this book. For the most up-to-date information about Canadian law schools, see the latest edition of the *LSAT Registration and Information Book—Canadian Edition*.

University of Alberta
Faculty of Law
Edmonton, Alberta
CANADA T6G 2H5

University of British Columbia
Faculty of Law
1822 East Mall
Vancouver, British Columbia
CANADA V6T 1Z1

University of Calgary
Faculty of Law
Calgary, Alberta
CANADA T2N 1N4

Dalhousie Law School
6061 University Avenue
Halifax, Nova Scotia
CANADA B3H 4H9

University of Manitoba
Faculty of Law
Winnipeg, Manitoba
CANADA R3T 2N2

McGill University
Faculty of Law
3644 Peel
Montreal, Quebec
CANADA H3A 1W9

University of New Brunswick
Faculty of Law
P.O. Box 4400
Fredericton, New Brunswick
CANADA E3B 5A3

University of Ottawa
Faculty of Law
57 Louis Pasteur
P.O. Box 450
Station A
Ottawa, Ontario
CANADA K1N 6N5

Queen's University
Faculty of Law
Kingston, Ontario
CANADA K7L 3N6

University of Saskatchewan
College of Law
Saskatoon, Saskatchewan
CANADA S7N 0W0

University of Toronto
Faculty of Law
78 Queen's Park
Toronto, Ontario
CANADA M5S 2C5

University of Victoria
Faculty of Law
P.O. Box 2400
Victoria, British Columbia
CANADA V8W 3H7

University of Western Ontario
Faculty of Law
London, Ontario
CANADA N6A 3K7

University of Windsor
Faculty of Law
Windsor, Ontario
CANADA N9B 3P4

York University
Osgoode Hall Law School
4700 Keele Street
North York, Ontario
CANADA M3J 1P3

Appendix D

LSAC Statement of Good Admission Practices

Introduction

This Statement of Good Admission Practices is designed to focus attention on principles that should guide law school admission programs. No attempt has been made to develop "legislative" guidelines, because no absolute rules apply to every situation. The statement is intended to improve the admission process in law schools and to promote fairness for all participants.

General Principles

1. The primary purpose of the law school admission process is to serve law school applicants, law schools, and the legal profession by making informed judgments about those who seek legal education. The responsibility that role carries with it demands the highest standards of professional conduct.
2. Law school admission professionals should avoid impropriety and the appearance of impropriety, as well as any conflict of interest or the appearance of conflict. They should not accept anything for themselves or the law school or pursue any activity that might compromise or seem to compromise their integrity or that of the admission process.
3. Law schools should strive to achieve and maintain the highest standards of accuracy and candor in the development and publication of print and other materials designed to inform or influence applicants. A law school should provide any applicant or potential applicant with information and data that will enable the applicant to assess his or her prospects for successfully (1) seeking admission to that school, (2) financing his or her education at that school, (3) completing the educational program at that school, and (4) seeking employment with degree from that school. If statistics are provided regarding admissions, financial aid, and placement, law schools should provide the most current information and should present it in an easily understood form. Significant errors of fact, as well as errors of omission, should be corrected promptly and prominently.
4. Law schools should establish application procedures that inform applicants of relevant criteria, processes and deadlines, respect

the confidentiality of student records and admission data, and provide for timely notification of admission decisions. Law schools should also ensure that all parties concerned with the admission process are familiar with and observe relevant laws, accreditation standards and institutional guidelines, including the Cautionary Policies Concerning Use of the LSAT and LSDAS developed by Law School Admission Council/Law School Admission Services (Law Services).

5. In making admission decisions, law schools should give special consideration to applicants who are members of cultural, ethnic or racial groups that have not had adequate opportunities to develop and demonstrate potential for academic achievement and would not otherwise be meaningfully represented in the entering class. Schools should also make reasonable accommodations to the special needs of disabled applicants. Law schools should make a special effort to provide the information noted in Number 3 above to those applicants who are members of minority groups or who are disabled.

Admission Policy

1. Law schools should develop coherent and consistent admission policies. The admission policies should serve law school applicants by clearly setting forth the criteria on which admission decisions are made and the manner in which the criteria will be applied.

Law schools should develop and promulgate concise and coherent admission policies designed both to regularize the admission process and to inform fully prospective applicants and prelaw advisors of the means used to select new law students. The policies should include consideration of the various criteria and processes used to make admission decisions, such as the Law School Admission Test (LSAT), prior academic performance, professional and other work experiences, equal opportunity considerations, disabled status, geographical diversity, letters of recommendation, personal statements, and personal interviews, if required. These and other considerations related to a law school's institutional mission or objectives may result in a preference for certain applicants. Each law school's admission policies should be adequately disclosed to all prospective applicants at the outset of the admission process.

Scores obtained on the LSAT and undergraduate grade point averages are factors by which applicants are judged by virtually all law schools. Law schools should ensure that all application materials accurately describe the manner in which LSAT scores, prior academic performance, and other factors are used in the admission process.

The LSAT is designed to measure some, but certainly not all, of the mental and academic abilities that are needed for successful law study. Within limits, it provides a reasonable assessment of these factors. LSAT scores provide at best a partial measure of an applicant's ability and should be considered in relation to the total range of information available about a prospective law student. Thus, the LSAT score should be used as only one of several criteria for evaluation and should not be given undue weight.

Use of cut-off LSAT scores below which no candidate will be considered is explicitly discouraged in the Law Services Cautionary Policies. However, a particular law school may discover evidence that applicants scoring below a certain point have substantial difficulty in performing satisfactorily in its program of studies. Based on that evidence, the law school may rationally choose to implement a policy of discouraging applications with LSAT scores below a certain point. Should a law school make that determination, applicants should be informed of that fact.

Similar considerations govern the evaluation of the applicant's prior academic record. Undergraduate grades are a significant indicator of potential success in law school. In addition to being one measure of academic ability, a strong scholastic record may indicate perseverance, organization, and motivation, all important factors which have few direct measures. There are, of course, measures of intellectual ability other than the cumulative grade point average. Unusual creativity, exceptional research skills, analytical prowess and other factors may not be reflected on a candidate's college transcript.

In evaluating the academic record, law schools may choose to consider factors such as grade inflation, the age of the grades, discrepancies among the applicant's grades, the quality of the college attended, difficulty of course work, and time commitments while attending college.

Law schools may also take into consideration additional factors when choosing among various law school candidates. Letters of recommendation often have a significant impact on admission decisions. Some schools believe that letters of recommendation are usually more candid when the subject of the letter waives access to them and recommend that applicants limit their rights to inspect this portion of their admission files. However, waiver of access to letters of recommendation or of any part of the student's record should not be made a mandatory prerequisite to admission. The Buckley Amendment specifically mandates that U.S. law schools must not require such a waiver.

As with members of cultural, ethnic, and racial groups, law schools should also recognize the importance of providing equal educational opportunity for disabled individuals. Sometimes the applicant's disability may prevent the assembly of a complete admission file. For example, some applicants can take the LSAT only under special conditions, making it difficult to interpret their test scores. Others may seek to have certain admission requirements waived entirely. In these circumstances, law schools can properly give weight to the disabled applicant's demonstrated ability to overcome obstacles in building a record of academic and professional performance.

Admission of applicants from a wide variety of academic, cultural, ethnic, and racial backgrounds, and the resulting diversity, enhances and enriches the educational experience of all students and faculty.

It is proper to prefer students who have taken courses such as those that develop skills in both written and oral communications, develop analytical and problem-solving skills, or promote familiarity with the humanities and social sciences to understand the human condition and the social context in which legal problems arise. The decision to prefer either a classical liberal arts education or a more narrowly focused one should rest within the sound discretion of the law school.

2. Law schools that accept transfer applications should state clearly the application procedures for transfer applicants and inform them of all relevant deadlines, necessary documents and records, courses accepted for credit, and, to the extent possible, course equivalency.

Recruitment and Promotion

1. Law schools are responsible for all people they involve in admission, promotional, and recruitment activities (including graduates, students and faculty), and for educating them about the principles of good practice outlined in this Statement, as well as all relevant laws, accreditation standards and institutional policies. Law schools that use admission management firms or consulting firms are responsible for assuring that these firms adhere to sound admission practices.

The oversight role entrusted to law schools includes supervision of all personnel involved in the admission process. Law school personnel, students and graduates who represent the law school at recruitment and other promotional activities should be informed of current law school programs and activities. They should be knowledgeable about the academic and financial requirements of attending the law school, and they should honestly and forthrightly respond to inquiries.

Professional recruiting organizations, though not formally affiliated with law schools, nonetheless are part of the admission process when they are engaged by law schools. Law schools engaging outside services are responsible for ensuring the integrity and the accuracy of the work performed for them. For example, errors or misleading statements appearing in recruitment brochures and law school catalogs may not be ascribed to the company performing the service. Law schools cannot abdicate the responsibility for accuracy by shifting blame to third parties.

2. Admissions publications should contain an accurate and current admission calendar and information about financial aid opportunities and requirements.

In addition to containing a complete listing of all relevant admission and financial aid deadlines, admission material should also convey accurate information about optimum dates, if any, for submitting admission materials. Among the items that might usefully be included are: dates for taking the Law School Admission Test; dates for submission of financial aid applications, including the best time for submission of materials to a financial aid need analysis service, if used; and the most useful date for submission of letters of recommendation. This information is particularly useful when law schools begin to make admission decisions prior to the deadline date for receipt of application materials under a "rolling" admission system.

Law schools should notify applicants about deadlines for financial aid applications and the criteria used in awarding aid. To the extent reasonably practicable, law schools should disclose how parental income will affect the financial aid determination. Similarly, the availability of need-based and of merit-based aid should be disclosed.

3. Law school admission professionals should be forthright and accurate in providing information about their institutions. Law school publications and any statements submitted for publication should contain current and accurate descriptions and representations of law school programs, campus life, and the surrounding community. Law schools should provide accurate, candid, and comprehensive information with respect to the law school opportunities sought by students and available to them.

Law school recruitment activities, e.g., law school forums, prelaw days, caravans, and law school fairs, provide an opportunity for law school representatives to engage in personal contact with applicants. In many instances, these activities are not only the first, but often the only direct contact applicants have with law schools until registration. In all of these instances, law school representatives should conduct themselves in a professional manner. Representatives attending these activities have an obligation to familiarize themselves with all aspects of the admission process at their respective schools. Recruitment activities should not include unreasonable and unfounded comparisons with other law schools.

4. Law schools should provide prelaw advisors and other educational and career counselors with accurate and appropriate information to assist them in counseling applicants about law school opportunities.

Issues of law school recruitment and enrollment require the cooperative efforts of college and university personnel working with law school admission counselors. Prelaw colleagues and other college counselors daily encounter students who are or may be interested in pursuing legal education. To serve the undergraduate population effectively, law schools should keep interested prelaw advisors, minority and other counselors informed of their admission requirements and institutional programs.

Application Procedures

1. Law schools should promptly notify applicants of admission decisions.
2. Law schools should respect the confidential nature of information received about applicants.

While a policy of openness and accessibility should form the basis for all communications with law school applicants, law schools should be scrupulous in maintaining the privacy of applicants. Without the expressed consent of the applicant involved and the author of the material in question, admission information relating to an applicant, such as LSAT scores, prior academic record, letters of recommendation, and dean's reports, should not be released to persons other than admission decision makers, the candidate and others with a legitimate interest in the admission process. This restriction would not prevent schools from sharing information that is not in a personally identifiable form, but even in this case, law schools should take care that the information is released with appropriate discretion.

From time to time, information about law school applicants at a particular law school is provided by Law Services. Information contained in many of these periodic reports is also confidential and should not be released to persons outside of the admission process, except as required by law.

3. A law school application should state clearly what information is being sought. The application should also state the applicant's obligation to provide accurate, current, and complete information. Further, the application should define the consequences of providing false, misleading, or incomplete information.

If the law school believes that false or misleading information has been provided by an applicant, that allegation should be submitted to the LSAC Misconduct in the Admission Process Panel for investigation. Then, if misconduct is found, all law schools to which the applicant has applied, or may apply, will be notified.

4. Except under early decision plans, law schools should not require applicants or other persons to indicate the order of applicants' law school preferences.

Law schools should allow applicants the freedom to explore as many opportunities to pursue legal education as possible. To preserve applicant options, law schools should not base admission decisions on the order of applicants' law school preferences, unless the school has established an early decision plan. An early decision plan is one under which an applicant and a law school mutually agree at the point of application that the applicant will be given an admission decision at a date earlier than usual in return for the applicant's commitment, at that date, to attend the school and withdraw all applications pending at other law schools, and not initiate new applications.

5. Except under early decision plans, law schools should permit applicants to choose among offers of admission as well as offers of scholarships, grants, and loans without penalty until April 1. Admitted applicants who have submitted a timely financial aid application should not be required to commit to enroll until notified of financial aid awards that are within the control of the law school.

6. No law school has an obligation to maintain an offer of admission if it discovers that the applicant has accepted an offer at another institution. Except under early decision plans, law schools should not suggest that acceptance of their offer of admission creates a moral or legal obligation to register at that school. Every accepted applicant should be free to deal with all law schools and to accept an offer from one of them even though a deposit has been paid to another school. To provide applicants with an uncoerced choice among various law schools, no excessive fee should be required solely to maintain a place in the class. Law schools should give applicants sufficient warning and ample time before withdrawing offers.

7. Law schools should maintain a waiting list of reasonable length and only for a reasonable length of time.

Law schools using waiting lists should ensure that the lists are of reasonable length and that final decisions about applicants placed on the waiting lists are made and communicated to the applicant as soon as possible.

Appendix E

Prelaw Readings: Books of Interest

The following list of prelaw readings offers prospective law students an overview of selected classics and current titles in certain subjects: law school and legal education, the legal profession, biography, and jurisprudence and legal issues. This list should not be construed as the official bibliography of Law School Admission Services; it is beyond the scope of this publication to provide any sort of definitive catalog of prelaw readings.

Some of these books have already withstood the test of time, and are as relevant today as when they were first written and published, generations ago. Examples are: Richard Kluger's *Simple Justice*—a rare glimpse into the private workings and deliberations of the Supreme Court; and Karl Llewellyn's *The Bramble Bush*—a classic study of how legal education shapes our legal institutions.

Other, more recent titles simply reflect the most current writing on the subjects listed above and are not necessarily recommended simply because they appear on this list. It will be up to you to search out the titles that pique your interest and make your own determination of their worth. The aim of our list is merely to give you a head start. We hope that those interested in pursuing legal studies will find the issues raised and the ideas discussed in these works helpful in making the decision to choose law as a career.

Law School and Legal Education

Barber, David H. *Winning in Law School: Stress Reduction.* 2d ed. Dillon, CO: Spectra, 1986.

Bay, Monica. *Careers in Civil Litigation.* Chicago: American Bar Association/Law Student Division, 1990.

Bell, Susan J. *Full Disclosure: Do You Really Want to Be a Lawyer?* Princeton, NJ: Peterson's Guides, 1989.

Bell, Susan J. *Interviewing for Success and Satisfaction.* Chicago: American Bar Association/Young Lawyers Division, 1989.

Calamari, John D. and **Joseph M. Perillo**, eds. *How to Thrive in Law School.* Pelham Manor, NY: Hook Mountain Press, 1984.

Carter, Lief H. *Reason in Law.* Boston: Little, Brown and Company, 1988.

Chase, William C. *The American Law School and the Rise of Administrative Government.* Madison, WI: University of Wisconsin Press, 1982.

Curry, Boykin, ed. *Essays That Worked for Law Schools: 35 Essays from Successful Applications to the Nation's Top Law Schools.* New York: Fawcett Book Group, 1991.

Deaver, Jeff. *The Complete Law School Companion.* New York: John Wiley & Sons, 1984.

Delaney, John. *How to Do Your Best on Law School Exams.* 2d ed. Bogota, NJ: John Delaney Publications, 1988.

Directory of Law School Joint Degree Programs. 2d ed. Washington, DC: Federal Reports, Inc., 1991.

Dutile, Fernand N., ed. *Legal Education and Lawyer Competency: Curricula for Change.* Notre Dame, IN: University of Notre Dame Press, 1981.

Dworkin, Elizabeth, Jack Himmelstein, and **Howard Lesnick.** *Becoming a Lawyer: A Humanistic Perspective on Legal Education and Professionalism.* St. Paul, MN: West Publishing, 1989.

Farnsworth, Edward A. *An Introduction to the Legal System of the United States.* 2d ed. Dobbs Ferry, NY: Oceana Publications, 1983.

Gillers, Stephen, ed. *Looking at Law School: A Student Guide from the Society of American Law Teachers.* 3d ed. NAL/Dutton, 1990.

Goldfarb, Sally F. and **Edward A. Adams.** *Inside the Law Schools: A Guide by Students for Students.* 5th ed. New York: Plume, 1991.

Goodrich, Chris. *Anarchy and Elegance: Confessions of a Journalist at Yale Law School.* Boston: Little, Brown and Company, 1991.

Hegland, Kenney F. *Introduction to the Study and Practice of Law in a Nutshell.* St. Paul, MN: West Publishing, 1983.

Kaplin, William A. *The Concepts and Methods of Constitutional Law.* Durham, NC: Carolina Academic Press, forthcoming.

Kelman, Mark. *A Guide to Critical Legal Studies.* Cambridge, MA: Harvard University Press, 1987.

Lasson, Kenneth and **Sheldon Margulies.** *Learning Law: The Mastery of Legal Logic.* Durham, NC: Carolina Academic Press, 1992.

Law As a Career: A Practical Guide. Newtown, PA: Law School Admission Services, Inc., 1993.

Llewellyn, Karl N. *The Bramble Bush: On Our Law and its Study.* rev. ed. Dobbs Ferry, NY: Oceana Publications, 1981.

Martinson, Thomas H., J.D., and **David P. Waldherr, J.D.** *Getting Into Law School: Strategies for the 90s.* New York: Prentice Hall, 1992.

Mayfield, Craig K. *Reading Skills for Law Students.* Charlottesville, VA: Michie Co., 1980.

Moliterno, James E. and **Fredric Lederer.** *An Introduction to Law, Law Study, and the Lawyer's Role.* Durham, NC: Carolina Academic Press, 1991.

Re, Edward D., and **Joseph R. Re.** *Law Students' Manual on Legal Writing and Oral Argument.* Dobbs Ferry, NY: Oceana Publications, 1991.

Roth, George. *Slaying the Law School Dragon: How to Survive—and Thrive—in First-Year Law School.* 2d ed. New York: John Wiley & Sons, 1991.

Stevens, Robert. Law School: *Legal Education in America from the 1850s to the 1980s.* Chapel Hill, NC: University of North Carolina Press, 1983.

Stover, Robert V. *Making It and Breaking It: The Fate of Public Interest Commitment During Law School.* Urbana, IL: University of Illinois Press, 1989.

Swygert, Michael I., and **Robert Batey,** eds. *Maximizing the Law School Experience: A Collection of Essays.* St. Petersburg, FL: Stetson University College of Law, 1983.

Turow, Scott. *One L.: An Inside Account of Life in the First Year at Harvard Law School.* New York: Penguin Books, 1978.

Vanderbilt, Arthur T. *Law School: Briefing for a Legal Education.* New York: Penguin Books, 1981.

Williams, Glanville. *Learning the Law: A Book for the Guidance of the Law Student.* 11th ed. London: Stevens, 1982.

Wydick, Richard C. *Plain English for Lawyers.* 2d ed. Durham, NC: Carolina Academic Press, 1985.

Legal Profession

Abel, Richard L. *American Lawyers.* New York: Oxford University Press, 1989.

Arron, Deborah. *Running From the Law: Why Good Lawyers Are Getting Out of the Legal Profession.* Berkeley, CA: Ten Speed Press, 1991.

Arron, Deborah. *What Can You Do With a Law Degree? A Lawyer's Guide to Career Alternatives Inside, Outside, and Around the Law.* Seattle: Niche Press, 1992.

Bailey, F. Lee. *To Be A Trial Lawyer.* New York: John Wiley & Sons, 1985.

Carey, William T. *Law Students: How to Get a Job When There Aren't Any*. Durham, NC: Carolina Academic Press, 1986.

Couric, Emily. *The Trial Lawyers: The Nation's Top Litigators Tell How They Win*. New York: St. Martin's Press, 1988.

Delaney, John. *Learning Legal Reasoning: Briefing, Analysis and Theory*, rev. ed. Bogota, NJ: John Delaney Publications, 1987.

Epstein, Cynthia Fuchs. *Women in Law*. New York: Basic Books, 1981.

Foonberg, Jay G. *How to Start and Build a Law Practice*. 3d ed. Chicago: American Bar Association/Law Student Division, 1991.

Galanter, Marc, and **Thomas Palay**. *Tournament of Lawyers: The Transformation of the Big Law Firm*. Chicago: University of Chicago Press, 1991.

Greene, Robert Michael. *Making Partner: A Guide for Law Firm Associates*. Chicago: American Bar Association, Section of Law Practice Management, 1992.

Henslee, William D. *Careers in Entertainment Law*. Chicago: American Bar Association/Law Student Division, 1990.

López, Gerald P. *Rebellious Lawyering: One Chicano's Vision of Progressive Law Practice*. Boulder, CO: Westview Press, 1992.

Luney, Percy R., Jr. *Careers in Natural Resources and Environmental Law*. Chicago: American Bar Association/Law Student Division, 1987.

Mayer, Martin. *The Lawyers*. Westport, CT: Greenwood Press, 1980.

Moll, Richard W. *The Lure of the Law: Why People Become Lawyers, and What the Profession Does to Them*. New York: Penguin Books, 1990.

Munneke, Gary A. *The Legal Career Guide: From Law Student to Lawyer*. Chicago: American Bar Association Career Series, 1992.

O'Neill, Suzanne B. and **Catherine Gerhauser Sparkman**. *From Law School to Law Practice: The New Associate's Guide*. Philadelphia: American Law Institute/American Bar Association Committee on Continuing Professional Education, 1989.

Shaffer, Thomas L. with **Mary M. Shaffer**. *American Lawyers and Their Communities: Ethics in the Legal Profession*. Notre Dame, IN: University of Notre Dame Press, 1991.

Shropshire, Kenneth. *Careers in Sports Law*. Chicago: American Bar Association/Law Student Division, 1990.

Stewart, James B. *The Partners*. New York: Simon & Schuster, 1983.

Thorner, Abbie Willard, ed. *Now Hiring: Government Jobs for Lawyers (1990-1991 edition)*. Chicago: American Bar Association/Law Student Division, 1990.

Utley, Frances, with **Gary A. Munneke**. *Nonlegal Careers for Lawyers: In the Private Sector*. 2d ed. Chicago: American Bar Association/Law Student Division, 1991.

Wayne, Ellen. *Careers in Labor Law*. Chicago: American Bar Association/Law Student Division, 1985.

Biography

Auchincloss, Louis. *Life, Law and Letters: Essays and Sketches*. Boston: Houghton Mifflin Co., 1979.

Baker, Leonard. *John Marshall: A Life in Law*. New York: Macmillan, 1974.

Barth, Alan. *Prophets with Honor: Great Dissents and Great Dissenters in the Supreme Court*. New York: Vintage Books, 1975.

Darrow, Clarence. *The Story of My Life*. New York: Charles Scribner's Sons, 1932.

Davis, Deane C. *Justice in the Mountains: Stories & Tales by a Vermont Country Lawyer*. Shelburne, VT: New England Press, 1980.

Davis, Lenwood G. *I Have a Dream: The Life and Times of Martin Luther King*. Westport, CT: Negro Universities Press, 1973.

Davis, Michael D. and **Hunter R. Clark**. *Thurgood Marshall: Warrior at the Bar, Rebel on the Bench*. New York: Birch Lane Press/Carol Publishing Group, 1993.

Douglas, William O. *Go East Young Man: The Early Years*. New York: Random House, 1974.

Douglas, William O. *Court Years, 1939-1975: The Autobiography of William O. Douglas*. New York: Random House, 1980.

Dunne, Gerald T. *Hugo Black and the Judicial Revolution*. New York: Simon & Schuster, 1977.

Frankfurter, Felix. *Felix Frankfurter Reminisces*. New York: Reynal & Co., 1960.

Griffith, Kathryn. *Judge Learned Hand and the Role of the Federal Judiciary*. Norman: University of Oklahoma Press, 1973.

Griswold, Erwin N. *Ould Fields, New Corne: The Personal Memoirs of a Twentieth Century Lawyer*. St. Paul, MN: West Publishing, 1992.

Howe, Mark deWolfe. *Justice Oliver Wendell Holmes*. Cambridge, MA: Harvard University Press, 1957 (vol. 1), 1963 (vol. 2).

Kahlenberg, Richard D. *Broken Contract: A Memoir of Harvard Law School*. New York: Farrar, Straus & Giroux, 1992.

Lynn, Conrad J. *There is a Foundation: The Autobiography of a Civil Rights Lawyer*. Westport, CN: Hill & Company, 1978.

Marke, Julius J. *The Holmes Reader*. Dobbs Ferry, NY: Oceana Publications, 1964.

Mason, Alpheus. *Harlan Fiske Stone: Pillar of the Law*. New York: Viking Press, 1956.

Murphy, Bruce Allen. *The Brandeis/Frankfurter Connection*. New York: Oxford University Press, 1982.

Nizer, Louis. *Reflections Without Mirrors: An Autobiography of the Mind*. New York: Doubleday, 1978.

Noonan, John T. , Jr. *Persons and Masks of the Law: Cardozo, Holmes, Jefferson, and Wythe as Makers of the Masks*. New York: Farrar, Straus & Giroux, 1976.

Pusey, Merlo J. *Charles Evans Hughes*. New York: Macmillan, 1951.

Rowan, Carl T. *Dream Makers, Dream Breakers. The World of Justice Thurgood Marshall*. Boston: Little Brown & Company, 1993.

Simon, James F. *Independent Journey: The Life of William O. Douglas*. New York: Harper & Row, 1980.

Thomas, Evan. *The Man to See: Edward Bennett Williams, Ultimate Insider; Legendary Trial Lawyer*. New York: Simon & Schuster, 1991.

Urofsky, Melvin I. *Louis D. Brandeis and the Progressive Tradition*. Boston: Little, Brown and Company, 1981.

Westin, Alan F. *Autobiography of the Supreme Court: Off-the-Bench Commentary by the Justices*. Westport, CT: Greenwood Press, 1978.

White, G. Edward. *Earl Warren: A Public Life*. New York: Oxford University Press, 1982.

Wigdor, David. *Roscoe Pound: Philosopher of Law*. Westport, CT: Greenwood Press, 1974.

Jurisprudence and Legal Issues

Bickel, Alexander M. *The Least Dangerous Branch: The Supreme Court at the Bar of Politics*. 2d ed. New Haven: Yale University Press, 1986.

Bickel, Alexander M. *The Morality of Consent*. New Haven: Yale University Press, 1975.

Burns, James MacGregor, and **Stewart Burns**. *The People's Charter: Pursuing Rights in America*. New York: Alfred A. Knopf, 1991.

Cahn, Edmond. *The Moral Decision: Right and Wrong in the Light of American Law*. Bloomington, IN: Indiana University Press, 1955.

Cardozo, Benjamin N. *The Nature of the Judicial Process*. New Haven: Yale University Press, 1921.

Dershowitz, Alan M. *The Best Defense*. New York: Random House, 1982.

Dershowitz, Alan M. *Taking Liberties: A Decade of Hard Cases, Bad Laws, and Bum Raps*. Chicago: Contemporary Books, 1988.

Finkel, Norman J. *Insanity on Trial*. New York: Plenum, 1988.

Howard, A.E. Dick. *The Road from Runnymeade: Magna Carta and Constitutionalism in America*. Charlottesville, VA: University of Virginia, 1968.

Irons, Peter. *The Courage of their Convictions: Sixteen Americans Who Fought Their Way to the Supreme Court*. New York: Penguin, 1990.

Kairys, David, ed. *The Politics of Law: A Progressive Critique*. New York: Pantheon Books, 1982.

Kirk, Russell. *The Roots of American Order*. Malibu, CA: Pepperdine University Press, 1981.

Kluger, Richard. *Simple Justice: The History of Brown vs. Board of Education and Black America's Struggle for Equality*. New York: Alfred A. Knopf, 1976.

Konefsky, Samuel J. *The Legacy of Holmes and Brandeis: A Study in the Influence of Ideas*. New York: DeCapo Press, 1974.

Lee, Rex E. *A Lawyer Looks at the Constitution*. Provo, UT: Brigham Young University Press, 1981.

Lewis, Anthony. *Gideon's Trumpet*. New York: Random House, 1964.

Lewis, Anthony. *Make No Law: The Sullivan Case and the First Amendment*. New York: Random House, 1991.

Pfeffer, Leo. *Religion, State and the Burger Court*. Buffalo, NY: Prometheus Books, 1984.

Pound, Roscoe. *Law and Morals*. South Hackensack, NJ: Rothman Reprints, 1969.

Rosenberg, Gerald N. *The Hollow Hope: Can Courts Bring About Social Change?* Chicago: University of Chicago Press, 1991.

Simon, James F. *The Antagonists: Hugo Black, Felix Frankfurter and Civil Liberties in Modern America*. New York: Simon & Schuster, 1989.

Sobol, Richard B. *Bending the Law: The Story of the Dalkon Shield Bankruptcy*. Chicago: University of Chicago Press, 1991.

Spence, Gerry. *With Justice for None.* New York: Penguin, 1990.

Tribe, Laurence H. *God Save This Honorable Court: How the Choice of Supreme Court Justices Shapes Our History.* New York: Penguin/Mentor, 1986.

Unger, Roberto M. *Knowledge and Politics.* New York: The Free Press, 1984.

van den Haag, Ernest, and **John P. Conrad**. *The Death Penalty: A Debate.* New York: Plenum, 1983.

Westin, Alan F. *The Anatomy of a Constitutional Law Case: Youngstown Sheet & Tube Co. v. Sawyer.* New York: Columbia University Press, 1990.

Williams, Patricia J. *The Alchemy of Race and Rights.* Cambridge, MA: Harvard University Press, 1991.

Wishman, Seymour. *Anatomy of a Jury.* New York: Penguin, 1987.

Appendix F

*Geographic Guide to Law Schools in the
United States (by region)**

*Population information is derived from the U.S. Bureau of the Census,
Population Division, Washington, DC. Data are accurate as of the 1990 Census.
City populations reflect the number of people residing in the city proper, not
the metropolitan area which would include outlying suburbs as well. Donald P.
Racheter, director of the prelaw program at Central University of Iowa, also
contributed data for these regional maps.

New England

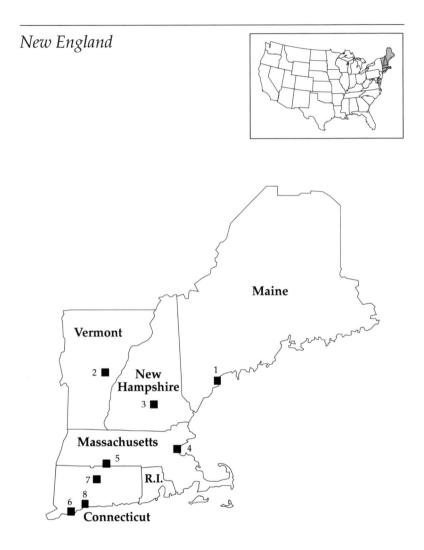

Maine

Vermont

2 ■

New
Hampshire

3 ■

1 ■

Massachusetts

5 ■

7 ■   R.I.

4 ■

6 ■ 8 ■
Connecticut

Maine
1 **Portland—Population: 64,358**
   University of Maine—Enrollment: 254/NA

Vermont
2 **South Royalton—Population: 23,089**
   Vermont Law School—Enrollment: 496/NA

New Hampshire
3 **Concord—Population: 36,006**
   Franklin Pierce—Enrollment: 399/NA

Massachusetts
4 **Boston—Population: 574,283**
   Boston College—Enrollment: 850/NA
   Boston University—Enrollment: 1,244/NA
   Harvard (Cambridge, MA)—Enrollment: 1,616/NA
   New England—Enrollment: 634/488
   Northeastern—Enrollment: 600/NA
   Suffolk—Enrollment: 1,020/670
5 **Springfield—Population: 156,983**
   Western New England College—Enrollment: 518/291

Connecticut
6 **Bridgeport—Population: 141,686**
   Bridgeport—Enrollment: 477/199
7 **Hartford—Population: 139,739**
   University of Connecticut—Enrollment: 435/222
8 **New Haven—Population: 130,474**
   Yale—Enrollment: 612/NA

"Enrollment" represents the numbers of total full-time/total part-time students. NA stands for "Not Applicable."

Northeast

New York

Pennsylvania

New Jersey

New York
1 **Albany—Population: 101,082**
Albany—Enrollment: 765/20
2 **New York City—Population: 7,322,564**
Benjamin N. Cardozo—Enrollment: 935/NA
Brooklyn—Enrollment: 1,045/394
Columbia—Enrollment: 1,025/NA
Fordham—Enrollment: 1,063/354
City University of New York—Enrollment: 457/5
The New York Law School—Enrollment: 901/483
New York University—Enrollment: 1,252/NA
St. John's University (Jamaica, NY)—Enrollment: 823/323
3 **Ithaca—Population: 29,541**
Cornell—Enrollment: 561/NA
4 **Buffalo—Population: 328,123**
State University of New York—Enrollment: 796/NA
5 **White Plains—Population: 48,718**
Pace—Enrollment: 490/424
6 **Syracuse—Population: 163,860**
Syracuse—Enrollment: 803/13
7 **Hempstead—Population: 725,639**
Hofstra—Enrollment: 827/NA
8 **Huntington—Population: 18,243**
Touro—Enrollment: 576/315

New Jersey
9 **Camden—Population: 87,492**
Rutgers–Camden—Enrollment: 600/150
10 **Newark—Population: 275,221**
Rutgers–Newark—Enrollment: 588/252
Seton Hall—Enrollment: 936/384

Pennsylvania
11 **Carlisle—Population: 18,419**
Dickinson—Enrollment: 518/2
12 **Pittsburgh—Population: 369,879**
Duquesne—Enrollment: 295/351
University of Pittsburgh—Enrollment: 708/11
13 **Philadelphia—Population: 1,585,577**
University of Pennsylvania—Enrollment: 688/NA
Temple—Enrollment: 908/399
Villanova (Villanova, PA)—Enrollment: 669/NA
14 **Harrisburg—Population: 52,376**
Widener—(see Delaware—Midsouth region)

"Enrollment" represents the numbers of total full-time/total part-time students. NA stands for "Not Applicable."

Midsouth

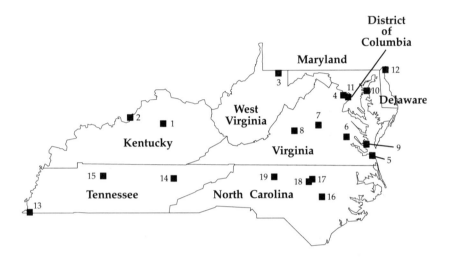

Kentucky*

1 **Lexington—Population: 225,366**
University of Kentucky—Enrollment: 459/NA

2 **Louisville—Population: 269,063**
University of Louisville—Enrollment: 426/106

West Virginia

3 **Morgantown—Population: 25,879**
West Virginia—Enrollment: 432/16

Virginia

4 **Arlington—Population: 170,936**
George Mason—Enrollment: 367/330

5 **Virginia Beach—Population: 393,069**
Regent—Enrollment: 300/0

6 **Richmond—Population: 203,056**
University of Richmond—Enrollment: 458/6

7 **Charlottesville—Population: 40,341**
University of Virginia—Enrollment: 1,155/NA

8 **Lexington—Population: 6,959**
Washington and Lee—Enrollment: 375/NA

9 **Williamsburg—Population: 11,530**
College of William and Mary—Enrollment: 545/NA

Maryland
10 **Baltimore—Population: 736,014**
University of Baltimore—Enrollment: 628/508
University of Maryland—Enrollment: 619/238

District of Columbia
11 **Washington, DC—Population: 606,900**
American—Enrollment: 269/99
Catholic University of America—Enrollment: 670/275
District of Columbia—Enrollment: 245/NA
Georgetown—Enrollment: 1,535/499
George Washington—Enrollment: 1,155/286
Howard—Enrollment: 453/NA

Delaware
12 **Wilmington—Population: 71,529**
Widener—Enrollment: 1,500/700

Tennessee
13 **Memphis—Population: 610,337**
Memphis State—Enrollment: 385/23

14 **Knoxville—Population: 165,121**
University of Tennessee—Enrollment: 473/NA

15 **Nashville—Population: 488,374**
Vanderbilt—Enrollment: 550/NA

North Carolina
16 **Buies Creek—Population: 2,085**
Campbell—Enrollment: 310/NA

17 **Durham—Population: 136,611**
Duke—Enrollment: 594/NA
North Carolina Central—Enrollment: 227/79

18 **Chapel Hill—Population: 38,719**
University of North Carolina—Enrollment: 683/NA

19 **Winston-Salem—Population: 143,485**
Wake Forest—Enrollment: 474/NA

*Northern Kentucky University—see Cincinnati, Ohio (Great Lakes region)

"Enrollment" represents the numbers of total full-time/total part-time students. NA stands for "Not Applicable."

Southeast

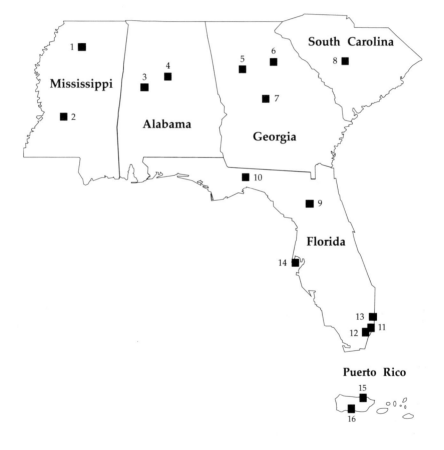

Mississippi
1. **Oxford—Population: 9,984**
   University of Mississippi—Enrollment: 513/1
2. **Jackson—Population: 196,637**
   Mississippi College—Enrollment: 378/NA

Alabama
3. **Tuscaloosa—Population: 77,759**
   University of Alabama—Enrollment: 547/NA
4. **Birmingham—Population: 265,968**
   Samford University–Cumberland—Enrollment: 634/NA

Georgia
5. **Atlanta—Population: 394,017**
   Emory—Enrollment: 730/NA
   Georgia State—Enrollment: 358/259
6. **Athens—Population: 45,734**
   University of Georgia—Enrollment: 619/NA
7. **Macon—Population: 106,612**
   Mercer—Enrollment: 405/3

South Carolina
8. **Columbia—Population: 98,052**
   University of South Carolina—Enrollment: 765/NA

Florida
9. **Gainesville—Population: 84,770**
   University of Florida—Enrollment: 1,150/0
10. **Tallahassee—Population: 124,773**
    Florida State—Enrollment: 613/NA
11. **Miami—Population: 358,548**
    St. Thomas—Enrollment: 476/NA
12. **Coral Gables—Population: 40,091**
    University of Miami—Enrollment: 1,172/193
13. **Ft. Lauderdale—Population: 149,377**
    Nova—Enrollment: 818/19
14. **St. Petersburg—Population: 238,629**
    Stetson—Enrollment: 673/NA

Puerto Rico
15. **San Juan—Population: 437,745**
    Inter American—Enrollment: 305/344
    University of Puerto Rico—Enrollment: 361/157
16. **Ponce—Population: 187,749**
    Catholic University—Enrollment: 670/275

"Enrollment" represents the numbers of total full-time/total part-time students. NA stands for "Not Applicable."

South Central

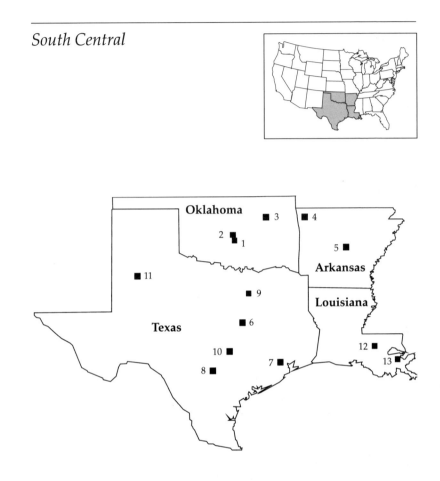

Oklahoma
1 **Norman—Population: 80,171**
University of Oklahoma—Enrollment: 678/NA
2 **Oklahoma City—Population: 444,719**
Oklahoma City—Enrollment: 415/237
3 **Tulsa—Population: 367,302**
University of Tulsa—Enrollment: 467/188

Arkansas
4 **Fayetteville—Population: 42,099**
University of Arkansas–Fayetteville—Enrollment: 435/NA
5 **Little Rock—Population: 175,795**
University of Arkansas–Little Rock—Enrollment: 261/132

Texas
6 **Waco—Population: 103,590**
Baylor—Enrollment: 424/NA
7 **Houston—Population: 1,630,553**
South Texas—Enrollment: 822/532
University of Houston—Enrollment: 966/285
Texas Southern—Enrollment: 568/NA
8 **San Antonio—Population: 935,933**
St. Mary's—Enrollment: 723/NA
9 **Dallas—Population: 1,006,877**
Southern Methodist—Enrollment: 772/NA
10 **Austin—Population: 465,622**
University of Texas–Austin—Enrollment: 1,500/NA
11 **Lubbock—Population: 186,206**
Texas Tech—Enrollment: 613/NA

Louisiana
12 **Baton Rouge—Population: 219,531**
Louisiana State—Enrollment: 785/NA
Southern—Enrollment: 331/NA
13 **New Orleans—Population: 496,938**
Loyola–New Orleans—Enrollment: 578/197
Tulane—Enrollment: 968/NA

"Enrollment" represents the numbers of total full-time/total part-time students. NA stands for "Not Applicable."

Mountain West

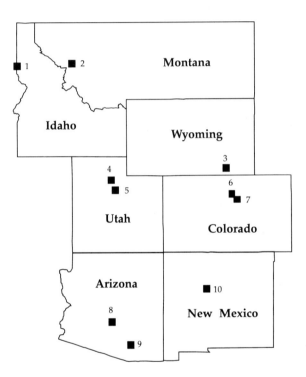

Idaho
1 **Moscow—Population: 18,519**
University of Idaho—Enrollment: 314/NA

Montana
2 **Missoula—Population: 42,918**
University of Montana—Enrollment: 226/NA

Wyoming
3 **Laramie—Population: 26,687**
University of Wyoming—Enrollment: 220/NA

Utah
4 **Salt Lake City—Population: 159,936**
University of Utah—Enrollment: 381/NA

5 **Provo—Population: 86,835**
Brigham Young—Enrollment: 489/NA

Colorado
6 **Boulder—Population: 83,312**
University of Colorado—Enrollment: 485/NA

7 **Denver—Population: 467,610**
University of Denver—Enrollment: 771/287

Arizona
8 **Tempe—Population: 141,865**
Arizona State—Enrollment: 532/NA

9 **Tucson—Population: 405,390**
University of Arizona—Enrollment: 480/NA

New Mexico
10 **Albuquerque—Population: 384,736**
University of New Mexico—Enrollment: 338/NA

"Enrollment" represents the numbers of total full-time/total part-time students. NA stands for "Not Applicable."

Far West

California

Nevada

■ 1

5 ■
■ 2

■ 3

■ 4

6

Hawaii

California

1 **Sacramento—Population: 369,365**
University of California–Davis (Davis, CA)—Enrollment: 481/NA
McGeorge—Enrollment: 850/375

2 **Santa Clara—Population: 93,613**
Santa Clara—Enrollment: 683/186

3 **Los Angeles—Population: 3,485,398**
University of California–Los Angeles—Enrollment: 942/NA
Loyola–Los Angeles—Enrollment: 1,050/316
Pepperdine—Enrollment: 719/NA
University of Southern California—Enrollment: 585/NA
Southwestern—Enrollment: 819/373
Whittier—Enrollment: 427/237

4 **San Diego—Population: 1,110,549**
California Western—Enrollment: 775/NA
University of San Diego—Enrollment: 711/224

5 **San Francisco—Population: 723,959**
University of California–Berkeley (Berkeley, CA)—Enrollment: 816/NA
University of California–Hastings—Enrollment: 1,253/NA
Golden Gate—Enrollment: 549/270
University of San Francisco—Enrollment: 531/137
Stanford (Stanford, CA)—Enrollment: 551/NA

Hawaii

6 **Honolulu—Population: 365,272**
University of Hawaii—Enrollment: 230/NA

"Enrollment" represents the numbers of total full-time/total part-time students. NA stands for "Not Applicable."

Northwest

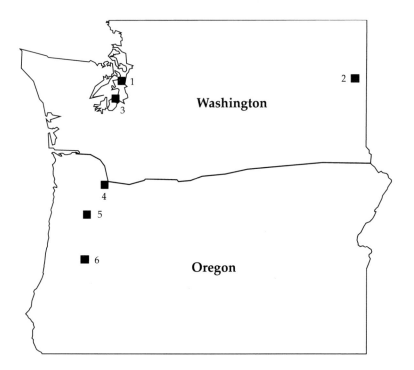

Washington

1 **Seattle—Population: 516,259**
University of Washington—Enrollment: 478/NA

2 **Spokane—Population: 177,196**
Gonzaga—Enrollment: 555/14

3 **Tacoma—Population: 176,664**
University of Puget Sound—Enrollment: 712/163

Oregon

4 **Portland—Population: 437,319**
Lewis & Clark—Enrollment: 451/241

5 **Salem—Population: 107,786**
Willamette—Enrollment: 468/NA

6 **Eugene—Population: 112,669**
University of Oregon—Enrollment: 436/NA

"Enrollment" represents the numbers of total full-time/total part-time students. NA stands for "Not Applicable."

Midwest

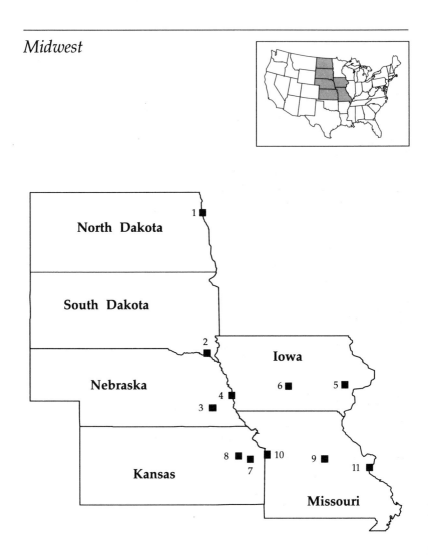

North Dakota
1 **Grand Forks—Population: 49,425**
University of North Dakota—Enrollment: 270/NA

South Dakota
2 **Vermillion—Population: 10,034**
University of South Dakota—Enrollment: 225/NA

Nebraska
3 **Lincoln—Population: 191,972**
University of Nebraska—Enrollment: 463/2
4 **Omaha—Population: 335,795**
Creighton—Enrollment: 575/17

Iowa
5 **Iowa City—Population: 59,738**
University of Iowa—Enrollment: 684/NA
6 **Des Moines—Population: 193,187**
Drake—Enrollment: 520/23

Kansas
7 **Lawrence —Population: 65,808**
University of Kansas—Enrollment: 546/NA
8 **Topeka—Population: 119,883**
Washburn—Enrollment: 435/NA

Missouri
9 **Columbia—Population: 69,101**
University of Missouri–Columbia—Enrollment: 465/NA
10 **Kansas City—Population: 435,146**
University of Missouri–Kansas City—Enrollment: 482/3
11 **St. Louis—Population: 396,685**
St. Louis—Enrollment: 551/267
Washington—Enrollment: 651/NA

"Enrollment" represents the numbers of total full-time/total part-time students. NA stands for "Not Applicable."

Great Lakes

Minnesota

1 **Minneapolis—Population: 368,383**
University of Minnesota—Enrollment: 796/NA
William Mitchell—Enrollment: 461/669

2 **St. Paul—Population: 272,235**
Hamline—Enrollment: 606/NA

Wisconsin

3 **Madison—Population: 191,262**
University of Wisconsin—Enrollment: 843/59

4 **Milwaukee—Population: 628,088**
Marquette—Enrollment: 498/5

Michigan

5 **Lansing—Population: 127,321**
Thomas M. Cooley —Enrollment: 109/1,427

6 **Detroit—Population: 1,027,974**
Detroit College of Law—Enrollment: 430/360
University of Detroit, Mercy—Enrollment: 900/NA
Wayne State—Enrollment: 486/218

7 **Ann Arbor—Population: 109,592**
University of Michigan—Enrollment: 1,117/NA

Illinois

8 **Chicago—Population: 2,783,726**
University of Chicago—Enrollment: 540/NA
Chicago-Kent—Enrollment: 609/372
DePaul—Enrollment: 710/290
John Marshall—Enrollment: 609/372
Loyola–Chicago—Enrollment: 733/132
Northwestern—Enrollment: 200/NA

9 **DeKalb—Population: 34,925**
Northern Illinois—Enrollment: 297/NA

10 **Champaign—Population: 63,502**
University of Illinois—Enrollment: 630/NA

11 **Carbondale—Population: 27,033**
Southern Illinois—Enrollment: 334/NA

Indiana

12 **South Bend—Population: 105,511**
Notre Dame—Enrollment: 583/NA

13 **Valparaiso—Population: 24,414**
Valparaiso—Enrollment: 515/34

14 **Indianapolis—Population: 731,327**
Indiana–Indianapolis—Enrollment: 511/325

15 **Bloomington—Population: 60,633**
Indiana–Bloomington—Enrollment: 614/5

Ohio

16 **Toledo—Population: 332,943**
University of Toledo—Enrollment: 459/176

17 **Cleveland—Population: 505,616**
Case Western Reserve—Enrollment: 679/52
Cleveland State—Enrollment: 620/386

18 **Akron—Population: 223,019**
University of Akron—Enrollment: 379/221

19 **Ada—Population: 5,413**
Ohio Northern—Enrollment: 436/NA

20 **Columbus—Population: 632,910**
Capital—Enrollment: 469/318
Ohio State—Enrollment: 650/NA

21 **Dayton—Population: 182,044**
University of Dayton—Enrollment: 485/0

22 **Cincinnati—Population: 364,040**
University of Cincinnati—Enrollment: 407/0
University of Northern Kentucky—Enrollment: 238/173
(Highland Heights, KY)

"Enrollment" represents the numbers of total full-time/total part-time students. NA stands for "Not Applicable."

Appendix G

*Geographic Guide to Canadian Law Schools**

*Population information was supplied by the Free Library of Philadelphia, Government Publications Office; the Canadian Consulate; the *Canadian Yearbook, 1990*; and *Canada Business Facts, 1992*.

Canada

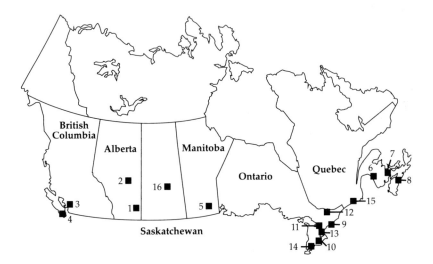

Alberta
1 **Calgary—Population: 636,104**
University of Calgary—Enrollment: 200/NA
2 **Edmonton—Population: 573,982**
University of Alberta—Enrollment: 500/NA

British Columbia
3 **Vancouver—Population: 431,147**
University of British Columbia—Enrollment: 710/10
4 **Victoria—Population: 58,718**
University of Victoria—Enrollment: 114/6

Manitoba

5 **Winnipeg—Population: 594,551**
University of Manitoba—Enrollment: 96/2

New Brunswick

6 **Fredricton—Population: 68,000**
University of New Brunswick—Enrollment: 240/NA

7 **Moncton—Population: 55,468**
University of Moncton—Enrollment: 111/NA

Nova Scotia

8 **Halifax—Population: 113,577**
Dalhousie Law School—Enrollment: 460/8

Ontario

9 **Kingston—Population: 55,050**
Queen's University—Enrollment: 465/16

10 **London—Population: 269,140**
University of Western Ontario—Enrollment: 473/NA

11 **North York—Population: 556,297**
York University–Osgoode Hall—Enrollment: 1,108/2

12 **Ottawa—Population: 300,763**
University of Ottawa—Enrollment: 562/8

13 **Toronto—Population: 612,289**
University of Toronto—Enrollment: 510/4

14 **Windsor—Population: 594,551**
University of Windsor—Enrollment: 417/10

Quebec

15 **Montreal—Population: 1,015,420**
McGill University—Enrollment: 542/NA

Saskatchewan

16 **Saskatoon—Population: 177,641**
University of Saskatchewan—Enrollment: 320/30

"Enrollment" represents the numbers of total full-time/total part-time or half-time students. NA stands for "Not Applicable."

Index

A

Academic record forms, 69
Academic assistance programs, 65
Accreditation, 51
Admission,
    factors affecting, 41
    profile grids, using, 67
    decisions, 89, 91
    process, 87
    index, 72
American Bar Association-approved law schools,
        Appendix B, 103
Applicant ages, 40
Applicants with disabilities, 49, 57
Application
    timeline, 70, 71
    Matching Forms, 69
    process, 68
Assessing chances of admission, 67
Association on Higher Education and Disability
        (AHEAD), 50

B

Bar exam, 94
Benefits of legal education, 14
Business, jobs in, 22

C

Canadian law schools, Appendix C, 114
Candidate Referral Service (CRS), 73
Candidate pools, 90
Career change, 8
Career services, 62, 95
Career satisfaction, 95
Categories of law schools, 52
Choosing law, 4
Choosing electives, 28
Civil procedure, 26
Clerkships, judicial, 22

Clinical courses, 28
Clinical-education programs, 63
Combined-degree programs, 64
Community activities, 41
Constitutional law, 27
Contracts, 26
Council on Legal Education Opportunity (CLEO), 50
Credit history, 84
Criminal law, 27
Criteria
    for admission decisions, 89
    for evaluating law schools, 55

D

Debt management, 84
Differences between ABA-approved and Non-ABA-approved
law schools, Appendix A, 51, 99
Disabilities, applicants with, 49, 57
Dual-degree programs, 64

E

Early decision, 88
Effecting social change, 14
Employment options, 18
Evaluating law schools, criteria for, 55
Evening programs, 55
Extracurricular activities, 41

F

Factors that affect admission, 41
Faculty/student ratio, 60
Faculty/student relationships, 60
Faculty, 59
Federal Work-Study, 84
Fee waivers, 72
Fellowships, 84
Financial aid forms, 82
Financial reward, 13
Financial aid packages, 83
Finding legal employment, 94
First year of law school, 24

G

Geographic locations of law schools in the United States,
    Appendix F, 133
Geographic locations of law schools in Canada,
    Appendix G, 155
Government, jobs in, 20
Grants, 84

H

HEATH Resource Center, 49
High school students and law school, 5
Highly competitive law schools, 52
Hold status, 91

I

Information, gathering of, 45
    about law schools, 47
Intellectual stimulation, 13

J

Job recruitment, 96
Judicial clerkships, 22

L

Large law firm, 19
Law schools
    list of ABA-approved, Appendix B, 103
    Canadian, Appendix C, 114
    local, national, regional, 53
    highly competitive, 52
    specialty, 54
    evaluating, 55
Law School Data Assembly Service (LSDAS), 69, 72
Law review, 29
Law School Admission Test (LSAT), 36 (see also LSAT)
Leadership qualities, 41
Legal research and writing, 27
Letters of recommendation, 75
Library, 61

Loan
    delinquency, 85
    default, 85
    repayment, 86
Loans, 84
Local law schools, 53
Location, 56
LSAC Statement of Good Admission Practices, Appendix D, 116
LSAT
    preparing for, 37
    score, 36
    retaking the, 39
LSAT/LSDAS Registration and Information Book, 69

M

Maps, Appendixes F and G, 133, 155
Military service, 43
Minority status, 42
Misconceptions, 17
Misconduct, 79

N

National Association for Law Placement (NALP), 96
National law schools, 53
Need analysis, 82
Nonlegal careers, 23
Notifying the law school, 93

O

Official Guide to U.S.Law Schools, The, 46

P

Parents and relatives, 5, 43
Part-time programs, 55
Paying for law school, 82
Personal statement, 73
Prelaw advisor, 46
Prelaw preparation, 31
Preparing for the LSAT, 37
Prestige, 14
Property, 26
Publications, 46

R

Ranking law schools, 51
Readings, prelaw, Appendix E, 125
Reasons to study law, 13
Regional law schools, 53
Required courses, 25
Returning to school after an absence, 40

S

Scholarships, 84
School size, 58
Schools, Appendixes B and C, 99, 114
Seat deposits, 92
Second and third years, 28
Site visits, 48
Small law firm, 20
Solo practice, 20
Student organizations, 66
Student body, 59

T

Torts, 26
Transcript
    request forms, 69
    evaluation, 34

U

Undergraduate
    education, course selection in, 32
    major, 33
U.S. law schools, Appendix B, 103

W

Waiting list, 92
Work experience, 42
Work-study, 84